The Rhode Island Campaign of 1778

From Washington Irving, *Life of George Washington*, III, 384

MAJOR GENERAL JOHN SULLIVAN

The

Rhode Island Campaign

of 1778

Inauspicious Dawn of Alliance

by

Paul F. Dearden

Published for
The Rhode Island Publications Society
by
The Rhode Island Bicentennial Foundation

Providence, 1980

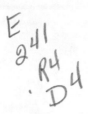

Copyright © Rhode Island Bicentennial Foundation 1980
All Rights Reserved
Printed in the U.S.A.
Library of Congress Catalog Card Number: 78-68920
ISBN: 0-917012-17-8

Cover illustration by Michael McGeough

For my Mother and Father
and
Dr. Patrick T. Conley

Contents

Illustrations

Preface

The armed confrontation that took place on Rhode Island and off its shores during the summer of 1778 is a subject which has held my interest since early youth, when I was presented with a copy of Katherine Pyle's *Once Upon a Time in Rhode Island,* first published in 1914 by the Society of Colonial Dames. Having undertaken the serious study of American history at Providence College, I first wrote an account of the Rhode Island campaign in conjunction with an undergraduate seminar presided over by Dr. Patrick T. Conley. Subsequently the resulting paper, in condensed form, became the subject of an article published in *Rhode Island History.* Still later my research was expanded to produce a master's thesis, also under the guidance of Dr. Conley, and it is that thesis, with some revisions, that forms the core of the present publication. It has been a fascinating search involving visits to numerous archives, as well as on-site inspections of the terrain on which the drama was played out.

The campaign is an event that has generally been ignored, or briefly noticed at best, by reputable historians of the American Revolution—a trend that has only recently begun to change. Increasingly, the story of the siege of Newport and the "Battle of Rhode Island" is being placed in its proper perspective in the history of the American War of Independence, with perhaps the best of the recent studies being Page Smith's *A New Age Now Begins,* the chief flaw of which lies in its unfortunate omission of authorities.

In contrast, the campaign has been given voluminous though often inadequate treatment by amateur historians and antiquarians of local vintage. Although some of their works are worthwhile, they generally fail to adequately analyze the events of the campaign itself, or neglect the national or international aspects of the struggle, while raising a number of serious historiographical questions.

One of the first professionally trained historians to begin dusting away the layers of myth covering the operations at Newport was George Athan Billias. Both in his article entitled "General Glover's Role in the Battle of Rhode Island," which appeared in a 1959 issue of *Rhode Island History,* and later in his superb *General John Glover and His Marblehead Mariners,* Billias disproved the long-standing assumption that it was Glover who, with his regiment of Essex County mariners, was responsible for the American army's successful amphibious withdrawal from Rhode Island following the campaign's failure. Indeed, Billias went so far as to establish that the famous Continental regiment which had evacuated Washington's army from Long Island, and ferried it to victory at Trenton, was no longer in existence in 1778.

Still other myths and misconceptions abound. The very question of the intensity of the fighting that took place during the Battle of Rhode Island is open to scrutiny. Various writers, most notably Samuel Greene Arnold in his *History of the State of Rhode Island and Providence Plantations,* and in a centennial oration commemorating the battle, published in *Rhode Island Historical Tracts,* assert that the encounter was particularly sanguine and speak in terms of a resounding American victory. This view has become the standard interpretation. Yet, a close examination of the facts leads to a quite different conclusion.

On a proportional scale, the fighting on August 29 was no more deadly than many of the Revolution's smaller scale encounters, and considerably less so than more well known actions. It must also be noted that no general overall engagement was brought on by either of the opponents, nor did they ultimately desire one. Both sides fed units into the fighting as the exigencies of a particular movement in a particular sector demanded. Indeed, a number of Pigot's units were retained within the lines about Newport throughout the better part of the day.

As to the viability of the assertion that the Battle of Rhode Island was truly an American victory, the harsh reality is that what General Sullivan's army managed to do was survive sporadic, though frequently strong, attacks by a foe intent upon harassing it, and then evacuate the island. All of this followed a costly and fruitless effort which the military and economic resources of New England and the Continent could ill afford, not to mention the ruinous effects on the morale of the already war-weary thirteen states.

Any discussion of the intensity of the battle must of necessity include an examination of the role played by the First Rhode Island Regiment, the so-called "Regiment of Slaves," which was in reality composed of not only slaves, but free Blacks, mulattoes, and Narragansett Indians, among others, forming an ethnic pastiche. Over the years the popular inveterately repeated version of the unit's stand in the little redoubt on the right of the American line has been one in which a small band of men repulsed a series of overwhelming enemy assaults at great sacrifice, thus saving the American line from collapse. This view became particularly prevalent during the Civil War and Reconstruction eras, with the appearance of tracts promoting, and memorializing, the service of Black men, both slave and free, as combat soldiers in the Union Army. Typical of these works are George Livermore's *An Historical Research Respecting the Opinions of the Founders of the Republic on Negroes as Soldiers* (Boston, 1863) and George H. Moore's *Historical Notes on the Employment of Negroes in the American Army of the Revolution* (New York, 1862). In truth, the newly recruited "green" troops did hold back a number of British attacks, but as these assaults swelled in intensity and took on a definite form, it became necessary for Nathanael Greene to engage the American right wing and ultimately hold that portion of the field where the redoubt lay. While the First Rhode Island made a contribution, it can hardly claim all the laurels for the defense of the American right.

Finally, and most intriguingly, I believe that there remains the question of the character of the Allied leaders as revealed in their personal conduct during the crisis in which they were enmeshed. Regarding the performance of Nathanael Greene, Lafayette, and d'Estaing, I believe that the following narrative speaks for itself. That of John Sullivan is far more open to controversy from an historiographical standpoint.

Some early volumes, such as the anonymously authored *Washington and the Generals of the American Revolution* (1859) and J. T. Headley's *Washington and His Generals* (New York, 1847), presented matter-of-fact accounts of Sullivan's career devoid of analysis, while generally apologizing for his failures and stressing his "patriotic" qualities. However, in his *History of the United States* (Boston, 1834–74) George Bancroft was extremely critical of Sullivan's career, and often savage in his characterizations. Bancroft's comments were in large measure responsible for generating the numerous filio-pietistic works concerning Sullivan by Thomas C. Amory, chief of which is *The Military Services and Public Life of Major General Sullivan of the American Revolutionary Army* (Albany, 1868). Throughout his writings, Amory is lavish in his praise of Sullivan, but presents little solid evidence on which to base his accolades.

The nature of Sullivan's leadership, and his personal qualities, have remained in dispute. In the 1930s the historical novelist Kenneth Roberts, a meticulous researcher, painted Sullivan in a highly unfavorable light in *Rabble in Arms*. Douglas Southall Freeman, writing in his multi-volume *George Washington* (1948–57), was less harsh but also found Sullivan lacking in many desirable traits.

The most balanced assessment of Sullivan appeared in 1961 with the publication of Charles P. Whittemore's *A General of the Revolution: John Sullivan of New Hampshire.* Yet, while often critical, even Whittemore's work is marred by his tendency to excuse Sullivan for some of his larger failings, both as a soldier and as a man.

One controversy, which stems from a particularly ironic episode in Sullivan's career in view of his conduct toward the French during the siege of Newport, has been laid to rest, however. In his *History* Bancroft alleged that as a delegate to the Continental Congress following his retirement from the army, Sullivan accepted funds from the French minister to the United States, the Chevalier de la Luzerne, in return for promoting French policy, especially as related to a prospective peace treaty. This assertion was vigorously assailed by Amory in *General Sullivan Not a Pensioner of Luzerne* (Boston, 1875), but has since been confirmed by Whittemore and thoroughly documented by William Stinchcombe in his *The American Revolution and the French Alliance* (Syracuse, 1969).

Whatever else may be said of Sullivan's career, it was a clear reflection of that of a genre of commanders who during the Civil War years, whether for good or ill, would come to be known as "political generals." As for the Rhode Island campaign, the events and issues connected therewith are a microcosm of the grayer, darker years of the War for Independence, which had at length become a conflict of flagging wills.

Paul F. Dearden

Providence
May 4, 1979

I

War Comes to Rhode Island

IN APRIL OF 1775 a British army column had been fired on at Lexington and Concord and very nearly decimated during the retreat back to its base at Boston, where the entire garrison was soon besieged. The long-festering political turbulence in the colonies had finally broken out in armed conflict. Passions ran high, and in June the Rhode Island Assembly deposed the Tory-leaning Governor Joseph Wanton and replaced him with the revolutionary-minded Nicholas Cooke.[1] Yet, Rhode Island was to witness more than the political consequences of revolution, and before the struggle came to an end, the state would pay a high price for its independence.

By the summer of 1775, Captain James Wallace, commanding a squadron of the Royal Navy composed of three ships of war, a bomb ketch, and eight tenders, began to strangle the maritime commerce of the rebellious Rhode Islanders. For an area that lived by its sea-borne trade, Wallace was more than an annoyance.[2]

Wallace intensified his activities in October when his ships bombarded the town of Bristol in retaliation for its failure to comply with his demands for provisions, which he sought for both his squadron and the beleaguered army at Boston.[3] That same month the General Assembly authorized the town of Newport to supply Wallace's ships, lest it suffer a similar fate.[4]

Having taught the inhabitants of Bristol a lesson in fidelity to their king, Wallace turned his efforts to other targets. His task was facilitated by Colonel Joseph Wanton, the son of the state's cashiered governor, who lent some of his Negro slaves to the captain to pilot the naval vessels around the island of Conanicut (now Jamestown) and point out houses that should be put to the torch.[5]

During the early hours of the morning of December 10, Wallace put his instructions to good use and landed on the island with some two hundred men, surprising the population while it slept. After a skirmish with a handful of defenders who turned out and were soon put to flight, Wallace's men pillaged and burned sixteen houses. As his prizes the captain carried off two prisoners and over a hundred livestock. Behind him he left smoking ruins and a badly wounded John Martin, who had stepped from his house to protest the attack to the British commander. For his efforts the unarmed Martin had a musket-ball tear into his stomach as he walked from his door.[6]

The coming of the new year brought no letup in Wallace's activity. On January 12 his men stormed ashore on Prudence Island and attacked a party of militia. In Wallace's own words, "we landed, beat them from Fence to Fence for four Miles into their Country, firing and wasting the Country as we advanced along. . . ." [7] Wallace, however, was stung the following day when he suffered three dead in a skirmish with the reinforced American contingent and was forced to withdraw from the island.[8]

The British captain continued his harassments until April. By then the evacuation of Boston by the British had diminished the usefulness of the Newport squadron, and its ships were dispatched to stations where the need for them was more pressing.[9] As for Wallace himself, he was ordered to Halifax in the *Rose* when batteries erected by the rebellious colonials on the surrounding hills made his base at Newport untenable.[10] Rhode Island's first harsh taste of war had thus come to an end.

The presence of Wallace, which caused the need to guard the shores of the colony, combined with the requirement of sending troops to Washington's army, had depleted Rhode Island's resources to the point where the General Assembly was forced to appeal for aid from the Continental Congress and neighboring states.[11] Yet the process of rebellion went on, and on May 4, 1776, the General Assembly declared that Rhode Island no longer owed allegiance to George III and his government. Now that assertion of independence would have to be defended, and the greater part of 1776 was spent in fortifying Narragansett Bay.

On May 20, 1776, this new feeling of confidence was boldly stated when a committee of the General Assembly, acting as a Council of War, wrote Congress that "the town of Newport is now capable of being defended against all the frigates in the British navy." [12] Again, on December 6 of that year, Governor Cooke maintained that with the aid of Connecticut and Massachusetts, Rhode Island would be able "to repel the Enemy if they should attempt to make a lodgement in this State." [13] Plans taking shape elsewhere were soon to prove the emptiness of the Rhode Islanders' confident assertions.

Notes

1. David S. Lovejoy, *Rhode Island Politics and the American Revolution* (Providence: Brown University Press, 1958), pp. 181–84.

2. Address of the Rhode Island General Assembly to the Continental Congress, January 15, 1776, in William R. Staples, *Rhode Island in the Continental Congress* (Providence: Providence Press Co., 1870), p. 54.

3. Captain James Wallace to Admiral Graves, October 14, 1775, in W. G. Roelker and Clarkson A. Collins 3rd, "The Patrol of Narragansett Bay (1774–1776) by H.M.S. *Rose,* Captain James Wallace," *Rhode Island History,* IX (January 1950), 20–21; Joel A. Cohen, "Rhode Island and the American Revolution: A Selective Socio-Political Analysis" (unpublished Ph.D. dissertation, University of Connecticut, 1967), p. 47.

4. John R. Bartlett, ed., *The Records of the Colony of Rhode Island and Providence Plantations,* 10 vols. (Providence: A. C. Greene and Bros., 1856–65), VII, 381–82.

5. Brigadier General Nathanael Greene to Samuel Ward, Sr., December 18, 1775, in Richard K. Showman, ed., *The Papers of General Nathanael Greene,* 2 vols. to date (Chapel Hill: University of North Carolina Press for the Rhode Island Historical Society, 1976–), I, 165–66.

6. Governor Nicholas Cooke to Rhode Island Delegates in the Continental Congress, December 12, 1775, in William B. Clark, ed., *Naval Documents of the American Revolution,* 7 vols. to date (Washington, D.C.: Department of the Navy, 1964–), III, 66–67.

7. Captain James Wallace to Admiral Graves, January 14, 1776, in Roelker and Collins, "Patrol of Narragansett Bay," *Rhode Island History,* IX (April 1950), 55.

8. *Ibid.*

9. Captain James Wallace to Admiral Graves, January 14, 1776, in Roelker and Collins, "Patrol of Narragansett Bay," *Rhode Island History,* IX (April 1950), 56.

10. Captain Francis Hutcheson to Major General Frederick Haldimand, April 24, 1776, in Clark, ed., *Naval Documents,* IV, 1222.

11. Address of the Rhode Island General Assembly to the Continental Congress, January 14, 1776, in Staples, *Rhode Island in the Continental Congress,* pp. 54–56; Irwin H. Polishook, *Rhode Island and the Union, 1774–1795* (Evanston: Northwestern University Press, 1969), pp. 13–15.

12. Council of War to the Continental Congress, May 20, 1776, in Staples, *Rhode Island in the Continental Congress,* p. 76.

13. Cohen, "Rhode Island and the American Revolution," p. 80.

II

The British Take Newport

AS THE SIEGE of Boston dragged on and imposed a forced inactivity on the British army, its officers began to consider other possibilities for a suitable theater of operations to which the seat of war might be shifted, thereby allowing the galling war of attrition to be brought to an end. In August of 1775 General John Burgoyne proposed the evacuation of Boston and the occupation of the island of Rhode Island. Two months later Sir Henry Clinton came to adopt much the same view.[1] Concurring with their judgment was the British commander, Sir William Howe. Writing to Lord Dartmouth, the Secretary of State for the American Colonies, on October 9, 1775, Howe reasoned that the occupation of Rhode Island would present a threat to Connecticut and impel that state to keep her militia at home for defense, thus depriving the main American army of one of its precious sources of manpower. In November Howe determined to take precisely that step. The ministry, however, disapproved, and the British army remained on the defensive.[2] On March 17, 1776, Boston was finally evacuated, and the British army sailed for Halifax. There Howe prepared a force to reconquer the rebellious colonies.

Shortly before Howe embarked upon his campaign, he informed Lord George Germain, Dartmouth's successor, that he would seize Rhode Island after he had captured the

5

expedition's principal objective at New York.[3] Although the newly arrived Wallace had brought word that the rebels were fortifying Rhode Island, Howe was not fazed. He informed Germain that "I do not apprehend they can prevent his Majesty's Troops from taking Possession of it, when the Strength of the Army will admit of a division for that important Service. . . ."[4]

Rhode Island offered an advantageous position to the British. There they would be a threat to the surrounding territory and simultaneously hold an excellent defensive position. In addition, Newport offered a fine harbor for the British fleet, which could raid the coast from Boston to New York.[5] The establishment of the blockade, designed to deprive the rebellious colonies of desperately needed supplies from abroad, increased the desirability of Newport as a roadstead, and Howe's brother, Richard, commander of the British naval forces in America, strongly advocated its capture.[6]

Throughout the summer of 1776 Howe had to delay his proposed move against Newport. With Washington concentrating his forces at New York, Howe simply could not afford to divide his command.[7] By the fall Wshington's army was running for its life, and Howe was finally free to strike at Rhode Island.

As commander of the expedition he chose the able but erratic Sir Henry Clinton, who opposed the venture, arguing that the approach of winter made the undertaking too dangerous.[8] Clinton also maintained that the troops could render better service in the pursuit and annihilation of Washington's fleeing columns in New Jersey. In short, Clinton believed that the war could be ended in one bold stroke. The Howes disagreed. Neither of them felt that the New Jersey campaign could end the war, and they wished to prepare a base for launching future endeavors in the colonies.[9] They also insisted that the harbor at Newport was necessary for the fleet's safety in the rough seas that winter would bring.[10]

Finally, on December 5, Clinton's seventy ships and transports set sail for Rhode Island under escort of Sir Peter Parker's squadron. With him, Clinton had two brigades of British and two of Hessian troops, totaling some six thousand men, plus Parker's thirteen warships.[11] The fleet reached the waters of Narragansett Bay on December 7, and at 4:00 P.M. Clinton dropped anchor four miles off Newport.[12] On the morning of the 8th, General Richard Prescott landed at Weaver's Cove with the Light Infantry, the Grenadiers, and the 10th Regiment. Prescott pursued the American militia to the northern end of the island, where it escaped via the ferries. He did, however, capture a few prisoners, a cannon, and some livestock that the Americans had attempted to take over to the mainland.[13]

Lord Hugh Percy landed with the heavy battalions and went to sustain Prescott, who had advanced with ease, while under cover of the warships the 22nd Regiment occupied the town of Newport and its batteries.[14] While the Americans had successfully removed most of their ordnance and many of the island's livestock, the fact remained that the town, which was "capable of being defended against all the frigates in the British navy," had fallen virtually without opposition.[15]

While the inhabitants of the island, the Quakers particularly, were highly discomforted by the presence of the Hessian regiments, Clinton maintained strict discipline among all his troops, and his efforts were largely successful.[16] On the day of the landing, a corps of "Safe Guards" composed of an officer and fifteen men from each of the brigades was formed under the command of a British captain to protect the citizenry and their property.[17] Despite all this, the usual atrocity stories spread, and one of them reached the ever-alert ears of the Reverend Ezra Stiles, who had fled Newport due to his association with the patriot cause. In his diary Stiles duly noted a tale that came out of Newport to the effect that "the Soldiers ravished two Lying-in Women." [18] It would not be the last such story, but in the ensuing struggle both sides would share in the practice of brutality.

Four days after occupying Newport, Clinton sent a captain and one hundred men of the 54th Regiment over to the island of Conanicut. In the words of Captain Mackenzie of the Royal Welsh Fusiliers, the detachment's assignment was to "take possession of it, and protect the Inhabitants." [19]

The capture of Newport had produced not only a naval base for the British, but it had also provided them with the extra dividend of bottling up the seven ships of Rhode Island's Commodore Esek Hopkins's Continental squadron, based at Providence. Parker was well satisfied that his efforts had "put an effectual stop to any further mischief from that nest of pirates." [20] Yet, as Massachusetts' General William Heath sagaciously noted, "Rhode Island was a great acquisition for the British, for quarters, forage, and a safe harbour; but lessened their ability for other more important operations in the field." [21]

Now that Clinton had Newport, he was forced to consider what his next step would be. General Howe had recommended that Clinton go on to capture Providence once he had secured the island of Rhode Island. Parker also advocated such a measure and offered to cover the landing of the troops. However, Clinton believed that the season posed too great a risk, and that a failure at Providence could endanger the remainder of his forces on the island. On Christmas Eve a severe snowstorm occurred, and on the following day all the senior officers, including Parker, agreed at a council of war that an attack on the mainland would be too hazardous.[22] In this General Howe concurred, writing to Clinton that "the season was too far advanced to attempt anything further." [23]

Before leaving New York, Clinton had received Howe's permission to return to England, but prior to his doing so Sir Henry instructed his successor, Lord Percy, that he should not attempt to leave the island for any military ventures until the coming of spring.[24]

Following Clinton's departure on January 3, 1777, Howe petulantly reversed himself and censured Clinton and Percy for not having moved against Providence. Howe also recalled part of the Newport garrison, stating that it was too large for its current purposes. He further commanded Percy to engage in any expedition on which Parker determined, whether he desired to do so or not. Percy, a veteran soldier who had saved the British column from annihilation on the road back from Lexington in 1775, was enraged and requested to be returned to England. Howe complied, and with Percy's departure Richard Prescott succeeded to the command at Newport.[25] Shortly Prescott would cause both the natives and his troops to wish once again for the days of Clinton and Percy.

With the coming of 1777 the prospects of the American cause seemed grim. On the Atlantic coast the patriots had lost two of their most important harbors with the seizure of Newport and New York. To the north the smallpox-ridden American army had been pushed out of Canada and just barely escaped destruction, while Howe's forces had succeeded in pushing as far up the Hudson River as the Highlands. Yet, there remained reasons for hope. In New Jersey, Washington had launched slashing attacks at Trenton and Princeton, giving American morale an inestimable boost, and then went on to elude Cornwallis's pursuit. On Lake Champlain, the energetic Benedict Arnold had halted Sir Guy Carleton's attempt to move down the Champlain Valley to the Hudson and link up with Howe, by making a desperate stand in a naval battle at Valcour Island on October 11, 1776. At least the war would go on.[26]

Notes

1. Sir Henry Clinton, *The American Rebellion: Sir Henry Clinton's Narrative of His Campaigns, 1775–82,* edited by William B. Willcox (New Haven: Yale University Press, 1954), p. 22, n. 8. For purposes of clarification, the island of Rhode Island is that on which the town of Newport is situated.

2. Troyer S. Anderson, *The Command of the Howe Brothers during the American Revolution* (New York: Oxford University Press, 1936), pp. 113–15.

3. Major General William Howe to Lord George Germain, April 25, 1776, in Clark, ed., *Naval Documents,* IV, 1248.

4. *Ibid.*

5. Piers Macksey, *The War for America* (Cambridge: Harvard University Press, 1964), p. 115.

6. William B. Willcox, *Portrait of a General: Sir Henry Clinton* (New York: Random House, 1964), p. 118.

7. Macksey, *War for America*, p. 87.

8. Clinton, *American Rebellion*, p. 54.

9. Willcox, *Portrait of a General*, pp. 116–19.

10. Clinton, *American Rebellion*, p. 56, n. 34.

11. *Ibid.*, p. 57; Frederick Mackenzie, *The Diary of Frederick Mackenzie, Giving a Daily Narrative of His Military Service as an Officer of the Regiment of Royal Welsh Fusiliers during the Years 1775–1781 in Massachusetts, Rhode Island, and New York,* 2 vols. (Cambridge: Harvard University Press, 1930), I, 118–20; "The Narrative of Lieutenant-General Sir William Howe," in Bellamy Partridge, *Sir Billy Howe* (New York: Longmans, Green and Co., 1932), p. 268.

12. Mackenzie, *Diary*, I, 122–23.

13. *Ibid.*, pp. 123–24.

14. Clinton, *American Rebellion*, p. 57; Mackenzie, *Diary*, I, 124.

15. *Ibid.*

16. Willcox, *Portrait of a General*, p. 122; Mackenzie, *Diary*, I, 126.

17. *Ibid.*, p. 124.

18. Ezra Stiles, *The Literary Diary of Ezra Stiles,* ed. Franklin Bowditch Dexter, 3 vols. (New York: Charles Scribner's Sons, 1901), II, 97.

19. Mackenzie, *Diary*, I, 126.

20. Willcox, *Portrait of a General*, p. 122.

21. William Heath, *Heath's Memoirs of the American War,* ed. R. R. Wilson (New York, 1904), p. 108.

22. Willcox, *Portrait of a General*, pp. 122–23; Clinton, *American Rebellion*, p. 57.

23. *Ibid.*, p. 65, n. 15.

24. *Ibid.*, p. 52.

25. Willcox, *Portrait of a General*, pp. 127–28.

26. Willard M. Wallace, *Appeal to Arms: A Military History of the American Revolution* (New York: Harper & Bros., 1951), pp. 85–87, 124–26, 133; John R. Alden, *A History of the American Revolution* (New York: Alfred A. Knopf, Inc., 1969), pp. 208–09, 276–83.

III

Rhode Island Responds

RHODE ISLAND'S REACTION to the British seizure of Newport was, of necessity, defensive in nature, for the state's regulars were with Washington and its resources were already severely strained. In an effort to prevent further enemy incursions, the militia was mobilized and distributed along the coast of the mainland. For the time being, an effort to force the British off the island was out of the question, despite the unrealistic urgings of William Ellery, a native of Newport and one of the state's delegates to the Continental Congress. Throughout the period of the British occupation of Newport, Ellery played the role of the "armchair-strategist," continually writing from Congress to urge his state to assume the offensive. In a letter to Governor Cooke dated December 25, 1776, Ellery stated his hope that

> the militia will universally turn out and not suffer the enemy to enter and ravage our State as they have done the Jerseys. I hope they will turn out in such numbers as to be able to give an effectual blow to the enemy in our quarters. If the army under Clinton should receive a mortal wound from the brave New Englanders, it would, in my opinion, bring the war to a speedy close. . . . There are brave, enterprising spirits in Providence. They burned a Gaspee. They may burn the British fleet. I hope they will make the trial, and every effort to destroy both the fleet and army.[1]

Unfortunately Ellery failed to perceive that the obstacle was not lack of American bravery or enterprise, but rather English military organization and strength, plus the very real factor of British naval superiority.

In the latter part of December, delegates from Rhode Island, Massachusetts, Connecticut, and New Hampshire met at Springfield, Massachusetts, to discuss the mutual problems of their states. There it was agreed that the other New England states would aid Rhode Island in her defense—a commitment beyond their ability to fulfill.

On the home front the General Assembly acted to streamline the state's political leadership to meet the urgent demands of war. Acting on December 10, the Assembly created a Council of War that was to rule when the legislature was not in session, and which was to consist of the governor, the deputy governor, and eight members of the Assembly.[2]

Responding to the British invasion of Rhode Island, Washington, who was unwilling to part with his chief strategist, Nathanael Greene, dispatched the elderly, rotund, uninspiring, and ineffective Major General Joseph Spencer of Connecticut to assume command of the American forces in the state. Washington also sent Brigadier General Benedict Arnold, possibly the most effective American combat officer of the war, to act as Spencer's second in command. Greene assured Governor Cooke, "Arnold is a fine, spirited fellow, and an active general." [3]

Spencer arrived during the last weeks of December, and Arnold reached Providence on January 12, 1777. Hungering for battle, Arnold immediately displayed the "active" nature that Greene had noted and quickly set about raising troops for an attack on Rhode Island's British garrison. Washington, however, urged caution and instructed him not to move unless success was "a moral certainty." [4] Arnold was further frustrated by Massachusetts's lack of enthusiasm for the project. Finally, troop demands in the Champlain Valley brought an end to his project.[5]

Now Spencer took an interest in an attack, despite the fact that he had only four thousand untrained militia to call upon.[6] His new-found enthusiasm agreed with the sentiment of the state's General Assembly, which passed a resolution in March urging Spencer to assault the island after raising volunteers for such a project on behalf of the Continental Congress.[7] This determination now placed Arnold in the position of opposing the expedition on the grounds that with such limited resources it could not succeed, and in arguing against it he came under severe and unwarranted criticism.[8] Spencer, however, relented, much to the disappointment of William Ellery.[9] In April, Arnold was released from his duties in Rhode Island and Spencer was left to his own designs. That same month Congress passed a resolution encouraging the states of Rhode Island, Massachusetts, and Connecticut to make a descent upon the British.[10]

While Spencer vacillated, one of his more daring subordinates did what he could to discomfit the enemy. On the evening of July 9, 1777, Lieutenant Colonel William Barton, a native of Warren and a hatter before the war had transformed him into a soldier, set out to capture the hated Richard Prescott. Acting in the fond hope that Prescott could be exchanged for his hero, General Charles Lee, who had been netted by a British raid at Basking Ridge, New Jersey, in December of 1776, Barton and a carefully chosen party of forty volunteers silently rowed past the British vessels guarding the western shore of the island of Rhode Island. After landing not far from the Overing House on West Main Road, where Barton knew that General Prescott would be passing the night with some of his female companions, the raiders quickly captured their quarry. Giving the amazed Prescott only time enough to put on his boots and gather his clothes, Barton's men dragged the general and his aide back to the whaleboats and managed to slip past the alerted British patrols and ships.[11]

The exploit both boosted American morale and flustered the British garrison.[12] In the words of Captain Mackenzie:

> They . . . executed it in a masterly manner, and deserve credit for the attempt. It is certainly a most extraordinary circumstance, that a General Commanding a body of 4000 men, encamped on an Island surrounded by a Squadron of Ships of War, should be carried off from his quarters in the night by a small party of the Enemy from without, & without a Shot being fired.[13]

Yet the larger project of driving out the invaders remained unaccomplished, and on August 21 the Continental Congress once again passed a resolution urging Spencer to descend upon the British.[14]

Throughout September Spencer made his preparations, but his activities did not go unnoticed by the enemy's new commander, Major General Robert Pigot, who had arrived in Newport on July 21.[15] Born in 1720, Pigot was a member of a distinguished military family and an able veteran of such savage conflicts as Fontenoy and Bunker Hill. The British general bided his time, strengthened his defenses, and readied his men for the attack that he was certain would come.[16]

On the night of October 19, Spencer postponed his invasion when he learned that the British had detected his boats crossing to the island.[17] Spencer assembled his forces once again on the night of October 26, but when a gale arose he gave up the attempt and the Council of War cancelled the expedition.[18]

By this time desertion had caused Spencer's force of militiamen to dwindle from 8,300 men to 5,000, and he had become exceedingly unpopular, especially with the Massachusetts troops.[19] That unpopularity caused some aspiring minor poet to place the following piece of doggerel in a conspicuous area of the camp, where the general found it upon emerging from his quarters in the morning:

> Israel wants bread
> The Lord sent them Manna—
> Rhode Island wants a head,
> And Congress sends a granny.[20]

The name "Granny Spencer" stuck.

The causes of Spencer's failure were investigated by both the Continental Congress and the Rhode Island General Assembly.[21] During this time the general made a desperate and discreditable attempt to place the blame for his bungling on sixty-one-year-old Brigadier General Joseph Palmer of Braintree, Massachusetts. Though both were exonerated of any wrongdoing and the weather was made the culprit, the humiliated Spencer offered Congress his resignation, which was accepted on January 13, 1778.[22]

Notes

1. William Ellery to Governor Cooke, December 25, 1776, in Staples, *Rhode Island in the Continental Congress,* pp. 112–13.

2. Bartlett, ed., *Records of the Colony of Rhode Island,* VIII, 56–57.

3. Nathanael Greene to Governor Cooke, December 21, 1776, in Showman, ed., *Papers of Greene,* I, 376.

4. James Thomas Flexner, *The Benedict Arnold Case* (New York: Crowell-Collier Publishing Co., 1962), p. 110; Willard Wallace, *Traitorous Hero: The Life and Fortune of Benedict Arnold* (New York: Harper, 1954), p. 123.

5. Flexner, *The Benedict Arnold Case,* p. 112.

6. *Ibid.,* p. 116.

7. Bartlett, ed., *Records of the Colony of Rhode Island,* VIII, 154–55.

8. Flexner, *The Benedict Arnold Case,* pp. 116–17.

9. William Ellery to Governor Cooke, April 6, 1777, in Staples, *Rhode Island in the Continental Congress,* p. 125.

10. W. C. Ford, ed., *Journals of the Continental Congress,* 34 vols. (Washington, D.C.: United States Government Printing Office, 1904–37), VII, 270–72.

11. William Barton's narrative of Prescott's capture, Rhode Island Historical Society Manuscripts, Vol. III, 13; Stiles, *Diary,* II, 182; Benjamin Cowell, *The Spirit of '76 in Rhode Island* (Boston: A. J. Wright, 1850), pp. 147–48.

12. Cohen, "Rhode Island and the American Revolution," p. 92.

13. Mackenzie, *Diary,* I, 150.

14. W. C. Ford, ed., *Journals of the Continental Congress,* VIII, 661–62.

15. Mackenzie, *Diary,* I, 156, 179–202.

16. *Ibid.,* pp. 177–202.

17. *Ibid.,* p. 196; Cowell, *Spirit of '76,* pp. 144–45.

18. *Ibid.;* Robert Richard Rudy, "Rhode Island in the Revolution" (unpublished M.A. thesis, University of Rhode Island, 1958), p. 28.

19. *Ibid.,* pp. 27–28; Cowell, *Spirit of '76,* p. 145.

20. Cowell, *Spirit of '76,* p. 145.

21. Staples, *Rhode Island in the Continental Congress,* p. 174; Cowell, *Spirit of '76,* p. 250.

22. Nathaniel N. Shipton, "General Joseph Palmer: Scapegoat for the Rhode Island Fiasco of October, 1777," *The New England Quarterly,* XXXIX (December 1968), 498–512, *passim.*

IV

The War Drags On

WHILE SPENCER HAD BEEN PREPARING for his ineffective effort against Rhode Island, the war in Narragansett Bay had settled down to a continuing series of rapid, vicious raids that kept both sides under constant tension. Typical was a raid launched by Lieutenant Colonel Sir John Campbell, who was to become an expert at this type of warfare. Early on the morning of August 5, 1777, Campbell led a force of 209 British troops in an attack against a battery at North Ferry on the Narragansett shore. The party succeeded in spiking the Americans' gun, taking four prisoners, inflicting eight casualties on the militia, and destroying four whaleboats, all with the loss of only one man.[1]

Certainly the Americans were not lax in their attention to this form of combat, nor were they any less adroit in executing it than were their British counterparts. On September 4, 1777, the brutality of the war was brought clearly into focus. That day the British frigate *Juno* sent a number of her boats to obtain water from the northern part of Prudence Island. While there, they were set upon by over one hundred of the enemy from the mainland. The Americans killed three of the Britons, wounded another, and took a midshipman and eight sailors prisoners. The raiders then escaped before the Royal Marines could land. Among the sights which greeted the rescue party was the body of a hapless seaman who had been shot three

17

times in the head, as well as in several other places, and muti-
lated with a bayonet.[2] Two years of war had hardened the an-
tagonisms on both sides.

The grimness of the war manifested itself in other ways as
well. Soon after the British occupation, Newport became a
haven for Loyalist refugees who had been forced to seek shelter from their "patriot" countrymen. Among those who
claimed the island's sanctuary was Rhode Island's deposed
governor Joseph Wanton and his family. Still others fled to
avoid service in the rebel army.[3] Yet, not all of those who
came to Newport did so under their own power, nor were they
as distinguished as Wanton. Two such men were Charles
Crow and Adam Steward of Boston, both of whom were seized
by their revolutionary neighbors in September 1777, tied to
carts, and "carted" through every town on the route to
British-held Rhode Island, where they were compelled to join
the enemy.[4] It is not without justice that the Revolution has
been called America's first "civil war."

Life for the patriot sympathizers on the island was no more
pleasant than it was for the Tories on the mainland. During
Spencer's proposed attack on Rhode Island many of the inhabitants of the island were arrested and placed on board the
garrison's prison ship, for as Captain Mackenzie noted, "they
have spoken their sentiments very freely of late."[5] Indeed, the
British were quite capable of resorting to subterfuge in order
to discover the enemies in their midst. Captain Mackenzie's
diary for March 25, 1778, gives a vivid example of this practice:

A party of Col° Wightman's Provincial Corps having disguised
themselves, and pretended to have just come over from the
Eastern shore, went last night to the houses of some of the Inhabitants of the East side of this Island, by whom they were
most favorably received, and where they fully discovered that
nothing but the dread of The King's troops prevents the
greatest part of the Inhabitants from joining the Rebels most
heartily in any enterprize against them. One of the Inhabitants
acknowledged that he was to have set fire to the Hay Magazine.
In short they all discovered their eagerness to inlist in the Rebel

Army, or to give them every assistance in their power. Three of
them were apprehended this day by the General's order, and
sent to The Provosts.[6]

For the King's troops the occupation was not overly grim,
but it had its elements of hardship. Sickness took its toll, but
not as heavily as it did on the natives, who were not as well
provided with fuel or fresh provisions.[7] In order to furnish
themselves with firewood, the British nearly denuded the island of its trees and tore down approximately sixty houses
outside of Newport alone.[8]

However, the tedium of occupation duty weighed heavily
upon the troops and drove more than one man to suicide.[9] Desertion was also prevalent, and Captain Mackenzie's diary is
filled with numerous instances of it, especially among the
Hessian regiments whose men were not always as well cared
for by their officers as were their British counterparts.[10] In addition, relations between the British and their German allies
were not always on the best footing. One Hessian officer has
recorded that when two British officers attempted to dispos-
sess him of his room and make it their own, it became necessary for him to show them the door with the point of his
sword.[11]

Added to all of these demoralizing factors was the ever-
present danger of a full-scale American assault upon the island. Soon this threat would become a reality.

Notes

1. Mackenzie, *Diary,* I, 161–62.

2. Mackenzie, *Diary,* I, 173.

3. *Ibid.,* p. 257.

4. Lorenzo Sabine, *Biographical Sketches of Loyalists of the American
Revolution,* 2 vols. (Boston, 1864), I, 343; *Ibid.,* II, 331.

5. Mackenzie, *Diary,* I, 198–200.

6. *Ibid.,* pp. 259–60.

7. *Ibid.,* p. 255; Edward J. Winslow, *The Hessians and the Other German
Auxiliaries of Great Britain in the Revolutionary War* (New York, 1884),
p. 217.

8. Howard W. Preston, *The Battle of Rhode Island,* Historical Publication Number 1 (Providence: State of Rhode Island and Providence Plantations, Office of the Secretary of State, State Bureau of Information, 1928), pp. 9–10.

9. Mackenzie, *Diary,* I, 146–47.

10. *Ibid.,* p. 239.

11. Letter from a Hessian officer to his brother, June 24, 1777, in William L. Stone, ed., *Letters of Brunswick and Hessian Officers during the American Revolution* (Albany: Joel Munsell's Sons, 1891), p. 210.

V

Sullivan, d'Estaing, and Hope

ON MARCH 2, 1778, General John Sullivan of New Hampshire wrote to Washington requesting leave from his duties at Valley Forge and the opportunity to return to his home in Durham, where he could recover from the "Fatigue" which he had suffered in the service.[1] While Washington declined to grant Sullivan the leave that he desired, he offered the New Hampshire general the command of the Rhode Island Department, as successor to Spencer. There, it was believed, conditions would be relatively tranquil and no great exertions would be required of Sullivan due to the defensive nature of the patriots' situation in the area.[2] Sullivan accepted the assignment, and on March 30 Governor William Greene of Rhode Island communicated to the new commander the state's satisfaction at his appointment, stating his hope that it would "prove equally beneficial to the public, and glorious to you."[3] Unfortunately, events were to make both the glory and the benefit nearly equal in their scantiness.

Following an overextended visit to his home in Durham, New Hampshire, Sullivan arrived in Rhode Island on April 17 and was received by Governor Greene and the council.[4] The following day the state Council of War formally placed all American troops within the boundaries of Rhode Island under the general's command.[5] On the whole the citizenry was impressed, and as former Governor Nicholas Cooke wrote Nathanael Greene, "I make no doubt he will give good satisfaction in this Department, It was more than we expected that Either you or he could be Spared, from the Grand Army." [6]

Yet, despite the population's initial pleasure at Sullivan's assignment to Rhode Island, his leadership was not an unmixed blessing. Tall, florid, stubborn, and often quarrelsome, Sullivan, while unquestionably brave, lacked the elements of military genius. As one of the foremost leaders of the revolutionary movement in New Hampshire and a delegate to the Second Continental Congress, Sullivan had quickly risen to political prominence and secured a brigadier generalcy in June 1775. During his botched handling of the latter stage of the Canadian campaign, his officers, and Arnold in particular, had just barely dissuaded him from making a suicidal stand at Sorel which would have left the path to the Hudson open to the British. However, despite his lack of promise in the field, he had remained popular with the New England congressional delegation. His political acumen helped him secure a promotion to the rank of major general on July 21, 1776.

At Long Island and Brandywine, his failure to carry out even an adequate reconnaisance of his positions had twice brought disaster to the Continental Army. His unsuccessful and costly raid against Staten Island on August 22, 1777, had led to his court-martial, and though acquitted, he had come under considerable criticism from his former congressional colleagues, particularly those from the Middle States, whose men had been the chief casualties of the operation.

In the words of Douglas Southall Freeman, Sullivan had been sent to Rhode Island "not because of any special fitness for the post, but because the New Hampshire general happened to be more readily available than any other officer of appropriate rank." [7] But, for the time being, Sullivan was the representative of the Continent's "Grand Army," and he was accepted as such by the people he had come to protect.

For all his faults, Sullivan diligently set about meeting the requirements of his post, and from the first he was beset by troubles. Upon assuming his position, the new commander found himself badly pressed for troops. As he wrote to Henry Laurens, president of the Continental Congress:

> We have not a man from Connecticut & but part of two Companies from Mass[a] Bay. Some few have arrived from New Hampshire & about half their Quota is on the March— . . . I have to guard a Shore upwards of ninety miles in Extent from Point Judith to Providence on the west & from Providence to Seconnet on the East against an Enemy who can bring all their Strength to a Point & act ag[t] any port they Chuse. . . .[8]

Indeed, the manpower situation in Rhode Island had long been critical, and early in 1778 the state had undertaken an unusual response to its problem. On January 1, 1778, Brigadier General James Mitchell Varnum, representing his fellow Rhode Island officers encamped at Valley Forge, wrote to Washington urging that Rhode Island's two undermanned Continental battalions be merged and that a group of officers be sent home to recruit a new battalion composed of Blacks.[9] In forwarding this proposal to Governor Cooke, Washington stated that it was his wish that the governor "give the officers employed in this business all the assistance in your power." [10]

In late February the General Assembly passed an act providing for the recruitment of slaves, whose masters were to be compensated by the state, and permitting the enlistment of free Negroes, mulattoes, and Indians in a "colored regiment" which was to be commanded by Colonel Christopher Greene, a cousin of Nathanael and a veteran officer.[11] In return for a slave's service for the duration of the war, he was rewarded with his freedom.

Governor Cooke confidently predicted to Washington that he expected the enlistment of over three hundred slaves.[12] Eventually his prophecy was fulfilled, but from February 23 to August 3 the state raised only seventy recruits from its new source of supply.[13]

However, not all of the state's Black population was enchanted by the newly devised road to "freedom," and some went so far as to seek asylum with the British army in Newport, thus avoiding service in the American forces.[14] If some slaves had qualms about the new policy, their masters, who were concentrated in the southern portion of the state, were even less satisfied. As Nicholas Cooke wrote to Nathanael Greene, "yr observation upon South Kingston in respect to the Negro Rigement is Very just they are not pleased with it at all and grumble a goodeal there is many disafected persons in that and North Kingstown and the towns round there. about 30 have gone over to the Enemy this Spring." [15]

Certainly, the use of Black troops was not a radical innovation on the part of Rhode Island. Since the beginning of the war Blacks, both free and slave, had served in the American army on an individual basis. In Washington's army there was an average of fifty Blacks in each battalion, and at the Battle of Monmouth his forces included at least seven hundred Blacks.[16] Before the summer of 1778 was over, Rhode Island's "colored" battalion had justified the case of those who had called for its creation.

While the new battalion was being formed and Sullivan was calling for troops from the neighboring states to defend his district, the fears of the enemy did much to aid the general's cause. Expecting the worst, Captain Mackenzie noted the belief of the British command that Sullivan's arrival in Rhode Island foreshadowed the long expected onslaught. On April 18 Mackenzie wrote of Sullivan's coming: "as he is an enterprizing spirited fellow, it is likely he will succeed in his endeavors to collect a sufficient body of men to enable him to make some attempt on this Island. . . ." [17] It need hardly be said that the British frame of mind did not displease the American commander, who informed Washington that "the Enemy are Busy in Fortifying the Island & are much afraid that we are about to attack them. I wish the Deception may continue." [18]

Yet, despite his weakness, Sullivan's mind turned to thoughts of offensive action. On May 7 he wrote to General

William Heath, commander of the Eastern Department based
in Boston, requesting the use of two mortars and two howit-
zers to clear the east and west channels of Narragansett Bay
of British vessels.[19] His plans were frustrated, however, when
Heath informed him that the weapons were required for the
defense of Boston.[20]

All the while, Sullivan occupied himself with gathering men
and boats and reconnoitering the enemy's position, a fact
which did not go unnoticed by the British.[21] In response,
Pigot, acting on the belief that Sullivan would—as rumored—
soon strike at the island of Rhode Island, determined to take
the offensive in an effort to force Sullivan off balance and prevent him from striking a blow.[22]

Having been informed of the presence of a considerable
body of stores at Warren by the town's British-born school-
master, a man named Holland who had previously been considered sympathetic to the Revolutionary cause, Pigot chose
Warren and Bristol as his targets.[23] At 3:30 on the morning of
May 25, five hundred British and Hessian troops, under the
command of the veteran marauder Lieutenant Colonel
Campbell, landed on Bristol Neck at a point between the
slumbering towns of Bristol and Warren.[24] There they divided
into two parties, with one marching to Warren and the other
to the Kickemuit River. On the banks of the Kickemuit the
raiders found and burned all but twelve of the seventy boats
assembled there following Spencer's abortive expedition. The
British completed their work at the river by putting the torch
to the Kickemuit bridge, a quantity of naval stores, a store-
house, a corn mill, some gun carriages, and one of the state's
new galleys, which the patriots were able to save after only
slight damage.[25] In Warren, Campbell's men discovered a
cache of military stores and a powder magazine located in one
of the town's residences, which they then burned. The resulting conflagration and explosion engulfed the town's meeting
house and six other dwellings. In addition, the British burned
a privateer sloop lying at anchor in the harbor and destroyed

an artillery park of five cannon.[26] As for the troops, they mixed business with pleasure as they intimidated the town's inhabitants and helped themselves to such items as watches, rings, buckles, shirts, and teapots, as was the wont of that age of warfare.[27]

From Warren, the British turned their line of march south to Bristol, which Campbell had been given orders not to attack if he found it occupied by an enemy force. However, luck was with him as Colonel Archibald Crary, commanding a detachment of three hundred men and Captain Nathaniel Pearse's company of artillery, both of which were quartered in Bristol, received exaggerated reports of Campbell's strength and fled the town, leaving it open to the depredations of the enemy.[28]

Elsewhere, more daring men were preparing to fight. When word of the British attack reached Providence, Colonel Barton, a native of Warren, gathered up nearly twenty horsemen and with Sullivan's permission went galloping off to Bristol Neck to rouse the country and gather a force that could hold the British in check until Sullivan could bring up the main portion of the army.[29] Just as the British were clearing Warren on their march to Bristol, Barton and the almost two hundred volunteers who had joined him, plus Colonel Crary's regiment, struck at them. In the ensuing skirmish Barton, cursing and urging his men on, raised himself in his stirrups, waving his sword wildly. As he did so, a bullet ripped through his right thigh above the knee and tore upwards into his hip, slamming him back in his saddle. Despite his wound he fought on, and not until the enemy had left Bristol did he allow himself to be attended to.[30]

Continually harassed in a running fight to Bristol, as the Americans sniped at them from behind stone walls and played upon their column with two three-pounders, the British nonetheless succeeded in entering Bristol and treating it as they had Warren.[31]

At Bristol a number of Tories had prepared a cask of punch

in order to give their allies a congenial reception, but the redcoats were in no mood for partying, and the kick of a British
officer's boot sent the cask spilling into the street and scattered the welcoming committee.[32] Here the British destroyed
several cannon and burnt a quantity of supplies, the town's
church, and twenty-two houses.[33] Nearly all the houses were
looted, and the British troops "made no distinction between
their Friends & Foes—some women who had been long noted
as their faithful friends, were compelled by the Bayonett to
Stand while their Buckles were taken from their Shoes, their
Rings from their Fingers, their Handkerchiefs from their
Necks, & c." [34] The sale in Newport of these items and those
taken in Warren would do much to supplement the meager
pay of the common soldier, whose lot was never a happy
one.[35]

Finally, by noon, the British withdrew in their boats under
covering fire from the *Flora* and *Pigot Galley* and their redoubt at Bristol Ferry on Rhode Island. In their excursion
they had taken sixty-nine prisoners, most of them civilians, at
a total cost to themselves of eleven wounded and two drum-
mers taken captive.[36] The American casualties included two
or three dead and several wounded.[37] As for Barton, he was
carried to a house in Bristol where the bullet was extracted
from his hip. For the next three months a lingering fever endangered his life, and even after his recovery he would never
again see active duty in the field.[38]

The British raid once again caused Sullivan to fear for the
safety of his charge. In identical letters to Meshech Weare,
president of the New Hampshire Council, and Jonathan
Trumbull, governor of Connecticut, he chided the two states
for failing to send him troops and lamented that he had less
than five hundred men, a fact which he believed had led the
enemy to attack the mainland. Lest the depredations continue, he urged that the states send him men as quickly as
possible.[39] In concluding his missives he bitterly noted that
"the Inhabitants of this State think themselves much

neglected by the other States and I fear have but too much Reason." [40]

Sullivan's fears were well founded, for on May 31 Pigot renewed his attack. This time one hundred men led by Major Edmund Eyre, who had served under Campbell in previous raids, struck at Freetown (now Fall River) at the mouth of the Taunton River, with the intention of destroying a number of saw mills and a stock of planks intended for building boats. Eyre easily drove off the guard of forty men who opposed the British landing and then put the torch to a saw mill, a corn mill, nine large boats, and nearly 15,000 feet of plank.[41] Following his initial success, Eyre advanced towards a bridge that led to the town and the other mills. Here the British encountered twenty-five men who posted themselves behind a wall and blocked their passage. In repeated assaults Eyre engaged this force for an hour and a half and then retreated to his boats, having suffered a loss of two dead and five wounded, while the Americans emerged unscathed.[42]

Pigot's efforts once again caused Rhode Island to call for aid. On June 2 Governor Greene wrote to Henry Marchant at Congress that "we are almost entirely neglected by our sister states" and wailed that if aid were not forthcoming "I dare to prophesy that it is very probable that this State will be out of the hands of the present possessors in a very little time." [43] Marchant and Ellery replied that they would do what they could to get Congress to apply pressure to the other New England states. Finally, on June 13, Congress passed a resolution requesting that the delegates of New Hampshire, Massachusetts, and Connecticut inform their respective states of the necessity of forwarding troops to Sullivan.[44] Yet the aid would be slow in coming, and when it did arrive it would not be under congressional impetus.

France had been eyeing the war in America with increasing interest. Humiliated by her defeat in the Seven Years' War, the French looked upon the American rebellion as an opportunity for revenge. Early in the war France initiated covert operations aimed at supplying the American rebels with military stores and money. The American commissioners in Paris, however, continued to insist that military intervention by France was needed to ensure victory over the British forces in America. After some hesitation, the French on February 6, 1778, signed a treaty of alliance. On March 13 the French informed the British government of the treaties and Britain severed diplomatic relations. The long-expected war was now only a matter of time.

Rather than risk a major naval engagement with the British, the French ministry determined to make a decisive seizure of an overseas theater of operations, and Admiral Charles Hector Théodat, Count d'Estaing, a favorite of Marie Antoinette, was not averse to persuading the queen to propose an expedition to North America with himself at its head.[45] D'Estaing had his way. In February the British government learned that his Toulon fleet was preparing to sail.[46] Yet the government did not act, for in London, Lord Sandwich, head of the Admiralty, and Admiral Keppel, commander of the British fleet in the English Channel, argued that the possibility of a Franco-Spanish invasion of the British Isles made it far too hazardous to dispatch a fleet to meet d'Estaing at Gibraltar and prevent his entry into the Atlantic.[47]

With his fleet of twelve ships of the line, four frigates, and four xebecs carrying four thousand troops, including two battalions of the famed Irish Brigade, composed of expatriate Irishmen in the service of France, d'Estaing sailed from Toulon on April 13. Finally, on May 16, the British sighted d'Estaing's force in the Straits of Gibraltar and could be certain that his destination was the Delaware, where he intended to blockade Admiral Howe's Philadelphia-based squadron.[48]

Following a lengthy delay in preparations, Vice Admiral John Byron, grandfather of the poet, put to sea with thirteen ships of the line on June 9 under orders to pursue d'Estaing. Three days after he left port, Byron's nickname—"Foul Weather Jack"—caught up with him, for his ships were scattered by a gale, and bad weather dogged him across the Atlantic. Moreover, his difficulties were compounded by the fact that a shortage of masts had compelled him to equip his fleet with old spars and secondhand rigging that gave way before the onslaught of the elements.[49] As a result, his first ship did not arrive in New York until July 30, and seven more reached there in August, but Byron himself did not drop anchor at New York until the end of September, after a stopover in Halifax.[50]

In a letter dated May 4, Lord Germain warned Sir Henry Clinton, now commander in chief of the American theater, of the possible threat presented to him by the Toulon fleet. This message, which Clinton received on the first of July, also informed the general that Byron would sail one month before he actually did. Unfortunately, no one in the government took the trouble to notify Sir Henry of the change in timing.[51] This lack of knowledge on the part of Clinton was critical, for in June he had abandoned Philadelphia due to an order from the home government that he detach eight thousand troops from his army, nearly a third of his total force, and send them to Florida and the island of St. Lucia in the West Indies. There they were to guard against possible French and Spanish incursions.[52] Fortunately for the British, Clinton delayed the southern movement; otherwise, the British would very likely have been caught in their transports when d'Estaing finally reached American waters.[53]

Throughout his passage across the Atlantic, d'Estaing's progress was retarded by the slowness of some of his vessels and the necessity of keeping his fleet together. In addition, the admiral's penchant for practicing naval maneuvers in mid-ocean and pursuing stray merchantmen further delayed the voyage. As a result, the fleet did not arrive off the Delaware until July 8. A difference of ten days would have found Admiral Howe's ships in the process of evacuating Philadelphia and enabled the French to blockade his forces in the bay, thus stripping New York of its naval defenses and leaving it exposed to an American attack.[54]

CHARLES HECTOR THÉODAT, COUNT D'ESTAING

Adding further misfortune to the voyage's length had been its unhappiness, a factor in which d'Estaing himself played no small part. Born in 1729, he had reached the rank of brigadier general by the age of twenty-seven, and his career had been an active one, though not brilliant. During the Seven Years' War he had fought in India and seen service during the siege of Madras. Following the war d'Estaing had been the none too popular governor general of San Domingo for two years. Forsaking the army, he had been appointed a lieutenant general in the navy in 1763 (a practice not unusual under the *ancien régime*) through the influence of his friend Louis, the Dauphin, father of the future Louis XVI.[55] In the words of one of the officers who served with him in his American campaign, "one might say that he quitted the land service too soon ever to be a good general officer and entered the Navy too late to attain any real success as a commander." [56] Indeed, the fact that a landsman had been placed at their head aroused no small amount of animosity toward the admiral on the part of his subordinates, and a base rumor gained currency in the fleet that the troops sailing with it had been placed on board the vessels in order to enforce d'Estaing's orders.[57] Adding to the admiral's lack of popularity with his aristocratic subordinates was his insistence that each of his ships carry at least three auxiliary officers (commoners who were restricted to certain lesser ranks).[58] Clearly, his situation was uncomfortable and, as a result, his actions could not be totally unfettered. The best that could be said was that the count's command included two of France's ablest sailors, Bougainville and Suffern, although the latter found much to criticize in d'Estaing's timid conduct of the latter stages of the American campaign.[59]

Having reached the Delaware and finding the enemy gone, d'Estaing sailed north for New York on July 9 in hopes of contacting the American army, replenishing his badly depleted provisions and water casks, and finding relief for those stricken with scurvy after the eighty-seven day passage. Two days later he arrived off Sandy Hook, but his troubles were not yet over. Anxious to replenish his supply of fresh water, d'Estaing ordered the pilot (who had come abroad in the Delaware) to guide the fleet inside the Hook. The navigator, concerned over the danger posed by the shallow channel, refused to obey d'Estaing's directive. Thus, the French admiral found himself alone and unaided off the coast of the ally whom he had come to help.[60] As he wrote later in his report to the Secretary of the Marine, Sartines, "we had no news; not a boat came from Long Island or from the Jerseys which we had understood were eager to help us."[61]

As one of the few alternatives left to him, d'Estaing personally undertook a scout of the neighboring shore, despite the heavy seas and wind. On landing he discovered that he had walked into the midst of a Tory community, and as he wrote later, "I began to think I would be the first victim of our difficulties."[62] Withdrawing from his uncomfortable surroundings, he made his way up the Shrewsbury River, still searching for fresh water, and then returned to his flagship, the *Languedoc,* after having lost an officer and four men when several small boats went awash.[63]

Finally, while camped at Haverstraw, Washington received definite confirmation of the fleet's arrival on the evening of July 14 in a letter from d'Estaing.[64] In it the Count offered Washington naval assistance and solicited the general's friendship, stating that "I will try to render myself worthy of it by my respectful devotion to your country. It is prescribed to me by my orders, and my heart inspires it."[65] As his words indicated, the count was wisely playing the diplomat as well as the military man.

On July 16 Colonel John Laurens, an aide to Washington, braved the rough seas to go out to the *Languedoc* from the Jersey shore. Laurens carried a letter from Washington promising to march toward New York and urging d'Estaing to attack Admiral Howe's fleet inside Sandy Hook, a plan upon which the count had already determined.[66]

Washington could not have chosen a better emissary. The son of South Carolina's Henry Laurens, president of the Continental Congress, young John Laurens was a tested veteran possessed of a strong moral character and courage tinged with a streak of recklessness that would ultimately cost him his life. Educated in England and at Geneva, he was fluent in French, and this, with his polished air, made him a logical choice as a representative. In addition, Laurens's attachment to his chief was described by Lafayette as "devotional." [67] Certainly he was taken with America's new ally, and he was soon writing that d'Estaing "has inspired me in the short acquaintance I have had with him, with uncommon respect." [68] Indeed, throughout the entire campaign, Laurens never wrote a word against the count personally.

Inside the Hook, Admiral Howe prepared to receive d'Estaing's attack and skillfully arranged his ships in a defensive line that would give him maximum use of his inferior firepower by using the shallow bar of Sandy Hook to mask his fleet from the French. Although his ships were manned and officered by more able sailors than the French, Howe was in the unenviable position of having only six 64-gun warships, ten frigates, and a number of smaller vessels with which to match a crushing French broadside from two 80s, six 74s, three 64s, a 50, and four frigates.[69] Yet the attack did not come, for despite d'Estaing's enthusiasm for an assault upon New York, the French had been unable to find a safe passage into Sandy Hook, even with the guidance of experienced pilots whom Washington's aide, Colonel Alexander Hamilton, had brought to the fleet.[70] Although d'Estaing went so far as to call an assembly of his pilots and offer fifty thousand crowns to the man who would lead him across the sand bar, he found no takers.[71]

Further complicating matters was the fact that Washington refused to formulate a plan of action until he could be sure that d'Estaing would be able to come to grips with Howe. Thus, d'Estaing and his ships lingered off New York while their water supply dwindled and cases of the dreaded disease of scurvy multiplied.[72] D'Estaing's feelings at this impasse are clearly described in a letter from John Laurens to his father, in which he wrote that the count "laments the insipid part he is playing—keeping the English fleet blocked up within Sandy Hook; and taking prizes within their view every day does not satisfy a man of his great ideas." [73]

Responding to the stalemate that had developed, the Americans began to cast about for an alternative target for allied efforts. On July 11 Congress, through its president, wrote to Washington suggesting that d'Estaing's force might be used either against New York or Rhode Island, and it is certain that the powerful New England faction was pushing for a move against the latter.[74] This proposal reached the commander in chief on July 17, and that same day, acting upon the advice of his chief strategist Nathanael Greene, he took the first step in preparing for a possible attack on Rhode Island.[75] Writing to Sullivan, Washington instructed him to raise an army of five thousand men by applying to the states of Massachusetts, Connecticut, and Rhode Island in Washington's name. Sullivan was also ordered to procure pilots who were familiar with Narragansett Bay, gather provisions and munitions, and collect boats for a possible descent upon Pigot's command. If the French turned toward Rhode Island, then Sullivan was to be ready; if not, his preparations for an attack on Newport might distract the British at New York and throw them off their guard.[76] In conclusion, Washington ended his dispatch with a polite rap at Sullivan for his haphazard manner of keeping in touch with his commander in chief, stating that "as I have heard from you but once or twice since your arrival at Rhode Island, I am much at a loss for the situation of matters in that quarter. Be pleased therefore to inform me in your answer to this." [77]

On the same day that he wrote to Sullivan, Washington drafted a letter to d'Estaing broaching the proposed venture against Rhode Island. This letter he dispatched with Colonel Hamilton and Lieutenant Colonel François de Fleury. Fleury was a French soldier of fortune who had more than proved his merit during the course of the war and had particularly distinguished himself during the battle of Red Bank in 1777.[78] Laurens returned from the fleet on July 19 with word that the admiral was already considering such a course of action, as the passage across Sandy Hook seemed unnegotiable.[79] There was simply no escaping the fact that while a British ship of the line drew twenty-two feet of water, its French counterpart drew twenty-seven—too much to cross the sand bar without the greatest of risks.[80]

Unfortunately for Allied plans, both Clinton and Howe had anticipated a move against Pigot if the attack on New York did not materialize. As early as July 10 Howe wrote Clinton that one of his goals in forming his squadron at Sandy Hook was that "of engaging the French admiral's attention, that the reinforcement may get to Rhode Island." [81] Yet, not until July 22, when troops from the Continental Army were already on the march to join Sullivan at Providence, did Washington suggest to d'Estaing that Long Island Sound, the route connecting Newport and New York, be blockaded. D'Estaing's fleet never attempted such a measure.[82] Taking advantage of his enemies' negligence, Clinton dispatched five battalions to Newport in the hope that should Rhode Island be attacked, the reinforcements would enable Pigot to hold out at least until the fleets of Byron and Howe could combine and sail to his relief.[83] On July 15 five provision ships and nearly two thousand troops under Major General Richard Prescott, who had been sent to succeed Pigot once the crisis had passed, arrived at Newport.[84] For the present, Pigot would have to defer his desired return to England. However, not all of the newly arrived troops found their situation particularly grave. In the eyes of Stephan Popp, a twenty-three-year-old Hessian recruit, his regiment's new post held certain compensating factors. Writing in his diary, he noted that "the women are very beautiful and shapely, and almost like gods in attractiveness. In beauty they have superiority in all America." [85] Soon Popp would have more serious matters to occupy his mind.

With success at New York now apparently out of the question, Washington put the new plan of operations into action on July 22, when at 2:00 A.M. the Continental brigades of Brigadier General John Glover of Massachusetts and Rhode Island's James Varnum, as well as Colonel Henry Jackson's regiment, set off along the road to Providence. A water route had been suggested but was quickly rejected as being too hazardous.[86] Varnum, a close friend of Nathanael Greene, was a competent officer, influential in local politics, and a lawyer by profession. Glover was a different case. A shipowner from Marblehead, the plucky little Irishman was a veteran of savage fighting in Washington's New York and New Jersey campaigns, and had been responsible for ferrying the army across the Delaware in 1776. As commander of the force Washington appointed the Marquis de Lafayette, who had arrived in the colonies the year before and easily earned a place of trust within the army and with Washington in particular.[87]

Lafayette was delighted with the prospect of his new assignment, for d'Estaing, a distant relation of the marquis, had offered him command of the French troops with the fleet, thus presenting Lafayette with the prospect of being the first commander to lead a joint Franco-American unit and gaining the honor that such distinction would bring.[88] As he wrote to Sullivan:

> Nothing can give me more pleasure than to go under your orders, and it is with the greatest happiness that I see my wishes on that point entirely Satisfied—I both love and esteem you, therefore the actions we'll fight together will be extremely pleasant and agreeable to me . . . for god's sake, my dear friend, don't begin any thing before we arrive.[89]

Lafayette also informed Sullivan of d'Estaing's offer to the young marquis that he lead the French as well as his own unit, and the unfortunate process that was to end their friendship and threaten the French alliance was begun.[90]

At 3:00 P.M. on the 22nd, d'Estaing's fleet, after waiting for the return of the *Chimére*, which the admiral had sent to convey France's new minister, Conrad Alexandre Gérard, to Philadelphia, weighed anchor and sailed south as far as the mouth of the Delaware in an effort to deceive the British as to their destination. The stratagem failed, for Howe was still inclined to believe they would strike at Newport, and on July 26 Pigot learned of d'Estaing's departure from Clinton and was warned that his command would probably be the Frenchman's next target.[91]

On the same day that Lafayette's column marched out and the fleet got under way, Washington sent John Laurens galloping to Sullivan at Providence with word that the expedition against Rhode Island was to proceed. Laurens arrived "in 48 hours over the worst, and in some parts the most obscure road that I ever travel'd." [92] But already the ill-luck that was to plague the campaign had begun to take hold. Indeed, Sullivan did not even receive Washington's letter of July 17, alerting him to the possibility of d'Estaing's coming, until the 23rd.[93] Delay was inevitable while Sullivan gathered his supplies and his army of militia, which Washington no longer limited to five thousand. The time lost would have fatal consequences.[94]

John Sullivan, the mercurial and often quarrelsome general who had yet to show outstanding military qualities, despite the flattery of his friends, had a compelling reason to succeed on this occasion. On July 23 Nathanael Greene wrote to Sullivan from White Plains congratulating him upon his new assignment and stating that "the expedition you are going on against Newport I think cannot fail of success." [95] Greene also pointedly warned Sullivan against failure. "Everything depends almost upon the success of this expedition. Your friends are anxious, your enemies are watching. *I charge you to be victorious.*" [96] If Sullivan was to be responsible for another defeat, it would further diminish his reputation, which had already come under severe attack in Congress, and might well mark the termination of his military career.[97]

However, Sullivan had cause to feel fortunate that he had received command of the expedition, for Greene informed him that "a certain Northern heroe [Gates], gave His Excellency [Washington] several broad hints that if he was sent upon the Newport expedition great things would be done. But the General did not think proper to supersede an officer of distinguished merit to gratify unjustly a doubtful friend." [98]

Certainly Washington held high hopes for the expedition against Newport, and as early as July 22 he was hoping that, at the very least, it could be followed by a blow at the vital British naval base at Halifax.[99] As he wrote later:

> If the Garrison of that place [Rhode Island] (consisting of nearly 6000 Men) had been captured, as there was, in appearance, at least a hundred to one in favor of it, it would have given the finishing blow to British pretensions of sovereignty over this Country; and would, I am persuaded, have hastened the departure of the Troops in New York as fast as their Canvas Wings could convey them.[100]

Undoubtedly, the bagging of Pigot's force, coming so soon after Burgoyne's surrender, would have had a serious effect upon Britain's will to carry on the war.

Rhode Islanders enthusiastically embraced the possibility of a combined Franco-American expedition against the British in Newport. As Congressman Henry Marchant wrote to Governor William Greene on July 11, alerting him to the congressional suggestion that d'Estaing sail against Newport, the people of Rhode Island would finally have an opportunity "to rid themselves at once by an easy effort, under the blessing of Heaven, of the worst banditti that were ever suffered to curse the earth." [101] At last a realistic means of freeing Narragansett Bay from the British stranglehold and eliminating a threat which drained the state's resources was at hand.

Notes

1. General Sullivan to General Washington, March 2, 1778, in O. G. Hammond, ed., *The Letters and Papers of Major General John Sullivan,* Collections of the New Hampshire Historical Society, Vols. XIII–XV, 3 vols. (Concord, N.H.: New Hampshire Historical Society, 1930–39), II, 27–29.
2. Washington to Sullivan, March 10, 1778, in J. C. Fitzpatrick, ed., *The*

Writings of George Washington, 39 vols. (Washington, D.C.: U.S. Government Printing Office, 1931–44), XI, 57–58.

3. Governor William Greene to Sullivan, March 30, 1778, in Hammond, ed., *Letters and Papers of Sullivan,* II, 31.

4. Charles P. Whittemore, *A General of the Revolution, John Sullivan of New Hampshire* (New York: Columbia University Press, 1969), p. 82.

5. Resolution of the Rhode Island Council of War, April 18, 1778, in Hammond, ed., *Letters and Papers of Sullivan,* II, 34.

6. Nicholas Cooke to General Nathanael Greene, April 19, 1778, Peck MSS Collection, Rhode Island Historical Society, Vol. IV, 44.

7. Douglas Southall Freeman, *George Washington,* Vol. IV: *Leader of the Revolution* (New York: Charles Scribner's Sons, 1951), p. 613.

8. Sullivan to Henry Laurens, May 3, 1778, in Hammond, ed., *Letters and Papers of Sullivan,* II, 47.

9. Varnum to Washington, January 2, 1778, in Bartlett, ed., *Records of the Colony of Rhode Island,* VIII, 641.

10. Washington to Cooke, January 2, 1778, in *Ibid.,* p. 640.

11. Bartlett, ed., *Records of the Colony of Rhode Island,* VIII, 358–60.

12. Cooke to Washington, February 23, 1778, in Jared Sparks, ed., *Correspondence of the American Revolution: Being Letters of Eminent Men to George Washington,* 4 vols. (Boston: Little, Brown and Co., 1853), II, 78.

13. Lorenzo J. Greene, "Some Observations on the Black Regiment of Rhode Island in the American Revolution," *The Journal of Negro History,* XXXVII (April 1952), 157–59.

14. Mackenzie, *Diary,* I, 257.

15. Nicholas Cooke to General Greene, April 19, 1778, Peck MSS Collection, RIHS, IV, 44.

16. John C. Miller, *Triumph of Freedom: 1775–1783* (Boston: Little, Brown and Co., 1948), p. 509.

17. Mackenzie, *Diary,* I, 268.

18. Sullivan to Washington, May 1, 1778, in Hammond, ed., *Letters and Papers of Sullivan,* II, 44–45.

19. Sullivan to Heath, May 7, 1778, in *Ibid.,* p. 50.

20. Heath to Sullivan, May 20, 1778, in *Ibid.,* pp. 53–54.

21. Sullivan to Heath, May 1, 1778, in Hammond, ed., *Letters and Papers of Sullivan,* II, 43–44; Mackenzie, *Diary,* I, 273.

22. *Ibid.,* pp. 275, 284; Clinton, *American Rebellion,* p. 102.

23. Erich A. O'D. Taylor, *Campaign on Rhode Island, MDCCLXXVIII* ([Newport], n.d.), sheet c; Virginia Baker, *The History of Warren, Rhode Island, in the War of the Revolution, 1776–1783* (Warren, 1901), p. 14.

24. Mackenzie, *Diary,* I, 284–85.

25. Sullivan to Washington, May 26, 1778, in Hammond, ed., *Letters and Papers of Sullivan,* II, 57–59.

26. *Ibid.;* Mackenzie, *Diary,* I, 285.

27. Baker, *History of Warren,* pp. 18–19, 50–63.

28. Wilfred H. Munro, *The Story of the Mount Hope Lands* (Providence: J. A. & R. A. Reid, 1880), pp. 211–12; Edward Field, ed., *The State of Rhode Island and Providence Plantations at the End of the Century: A History,* 3 vols. (Boston: Mason Publishing Co., 1902), I, 485.

29. *Ibid.,* I, 486; Munro, *Mount Hope Lands,* p. 216.

30. Field, ed., *State of Rhode Island,* I, 486; Catherine R. Williams, *Biography of Revolutionary Heroes, Containing the Life of Brigadier General William Barton, and Also of Stephen Olney* (Providence, 1839), pp. 76–78.

31. Mackenzie, *Diary,* I, 287.

32. Munro, *Mount Hope Lands,* pp. 213–14.

33. Mackenzie, *Diary,* I, 283; Sullivan to Washington, May 26, 1778, in Hammond, ed., *Letters and Papers of Sullivan,* II, 57.

34. *Ibid.* It should be noted that such accounts are by no means always exaggerated, for it was precisely such conduct on the part of British troops, and especially their German allies, that helped to dampen the "Loyalist" rising that the North administration counted on to help win the war for England.

35. Fleet S. Greene, "Newport in the Hands of the British: A Diary of the Revolution," *The Historical Magazine,* IV (March 1860), 70.

36. Mackenzie, *Diary,* I, 286.

37. Sullivan to Washington, May 26, 1778, in Hammond, ed., *Letters and Papers of Sullivan,* II, 58.

38. Frederick H. Swan, *General William Barton: A Biographical Sketch* (Providence: The Roger Wiiliams Press, 1947), p. 22.

39. Sullivan to Meshech Weare, May 26, 1778, and to Jonathan Trumbull, May 26, 1778, in Hammond, ed., *Letters and Papers of Sullivan,* II, 55–56.

40. Sullivan to Meshech Weare, May 26, 1778, and to Jonathan Trumbull, May 26, 1778, in Hammond, ed., *Letters and Papers of Sullivan,* II, 56.

41. Mackenzie, *Diary,* I, 289–90.

42. Mackenzie, *Diary,* I, 290; Sullivan to Henry Laurens, May 31, 1778, in Hammond, ed., *Letters and Papers of Sullivan,* II, 62–63; *New Hampshire Gazette,* June 16, 1778, in Frank Moore, ed., *Diary of the American Revolution,* 2 vols. (New York: C. Scribner, 1860), II, 59.

43. Governor Greene to Henry Marchant, June 2, 1778, in Staples, *Rhode Island in the Continental Congress,* p. 183.

44. Messrs. Ellery and Marchant to Governor Greene, June 8, 1778, in Staples, *Rhode Island in the Continental Congress,* p. 284; Ford, ed., *Journals of the Continental Congress,* XI, 605.

45. Macksey, *War for America,* pp. 190–91; George Bancroft, *History of the United States,* 10 vols. (Boston: Little, Brown and Co., 1834–74), IV, 145.

46. Willcox, *Portrait of a General,* p. 215.

47. Macksey, *War for America,* p. 195.

48. Washington to Governor George Clinton, July 11, 1778, in Fitzpatrick, ed., *Writings of Washington,* XII, 171; Heath, *Heath's Memoirs,* p. 200; Mackenzie, *Diary,* II, 342; Asa Bird Gardiner, *The Battle of Rhode Island* (Providence: Society of the Cincinnati, 1911), p. 4; Macksey, *War for America,* p. 201; Gardner W. Allen, *A Naval History of the American Revolution,* 2 vols. (Boston, 1913), I, 328.

49. Nathan Miller, *Sea of Glory: The Continental Navy Fights for Independence, 1775–1783* (New York: David McKay Co., 1974), pp. 330–31; Macksey, *War for America,* pp. 198–202.

50. *Ibid.,* p. 212.

51. Clinton, *American Rebellion,* p. 381; Willcox, *Portrait of a General,* p. 217.

52. Macksey, *War for America,* p. 214.

53. *Ibid.,* p. 215.

54. Allen, *Naval History,* I, 328; James Buck Perkins, *France in the American Revolution* (Boston, 1911), pp. 261–62; Willcox, *Portrait of a General,* p. 237; Christopher Ward, *The War of the Revolution,* ed. J. R. Alden, 2 vols. (New York: Macmillan Co., 1952), II, 587.

55. Mark M. Boatner, *Encyclopedia of the American Revolution* (New York: David McKay Co., 1966), pp. 349–50; Perkins, *France in the American Revolution,* p. 259; Taylor, *Campaign on Rhode Island,* sheet d.

56. Douglas Southall Freeman, *George Washington,* Vol. V: *Victory with the Help of France* (New York: Charles Scribner's Sons, 1952), p. 504.

57. John Laurens to Washington, August 23, 1778, in Sparks, ed., *Letters to Washington,* II, 179–81; Taylor, *Campaign on Rhode Island,* sheet d.

58. Jonathan R. Dull, *The French Navy and American Independence: A Study of Arms and Diplomacy, 1774–1787* (Princeton: Princeton University Press, 1975), p. 145.

59. Alfred Thayer Mahan, *The Influence of Seapower Upon History, 1660–1783* (Boston: Little, Brown & Co., 1890), pp. 323–28.

60. Freeman, *Washington,* V, 48–49.

61. Freeman, *Washington,* V, 49.

62. *Ibid.*

63. *Ibid.*

64. *Ibid.,* p. 48.

65. D'Estaing to Washington, July 13, 1778, in Sparks, ed., *Letters to Washington,* II, 156–58.

66. Freeman, *Washington,* V, 47–48; Dudley W. Knox, *The Naval Genius of George Washington* (Boston: Houghton Mifflin Co., 1932), p. 46.

67. Alexander Graydon, *Memoirs of His Own Time with Reminiscences of the Men and Events of the Revolution,* ed. John Stockton Littell (Philadelphia: Lindsay & Blakiston, 1846), p. 476.

68. John Laurens to Henry Laurens, July 18, 1778, in John Laurens, *The Army Correspondence of Colonel John Laurens in the Years 1777–1778: Now First Printed from Original Letters to His Father, Henry Laurens, President of the Congress, with a Memoir by William Gilmore Simms* (New York: Bradford Club, 1867), p. 208.

69. Ira D. Gruber, "Richard Lord Howe: Admiral As Peacemaker," in *George Washington's Opponents,* ed. George Athan Billias (New York: William Morrow and Co., 1969), p. 249; Mahan, *Influence of Seapower,* p. 318; Dull, *The French Navy,* pp. 359–60.

70. Washington to d'Estaing, July 17, 1778, in Fitzpatrick, ed., *Writings of Washington,* XII, 185–87; Freeman, *Washington,* V, 49.

71. D'Estaing to Washington, August 3, 1778, in Sparks, ed., *Letters to Washington,* II, 171.

72. Freeman, *Washington,* V, 49–50.

73. John Laurens to Henry Laurens, July 18, 1778, in Laurens, *Army Correspondence,* p. 208.

74. Henry Laurens to Washington, July 11, 1778, in Edmund Cody Burnett, ed., *Letters to Members of the Continental Congress,* 8 vols. (Washington, D.C.: Carnegie Institute of Washington, 1921–38), III, 324–25; Rudy, "Rhode Island in the Reovlution," p. 79.

75. Nathanael Greene to Washington, July [n.d.], 1778, in George Washington Greene, *The Life of Nathanael Greene, Major General in the Army of the Revolution,* 3 vols. (New York: Hurd and Houghton, 1867–71), II, 98–99.

76. Washington to Sullivan, July 17, 1778, in Hammond, ed., *Letters and Papers of Sullivan,* II, 89–90.

77. *Ibid.,* p. 90.

78. Washington to d'Estaing, July 17, 1778, in Fitzpatrick, ed., *Writings of Washington,* XII, pp. 185–87; Freeman, *Washington,* V, 50.

79. Freeman, *Washington,* V, 50–51.

80. James Thomas Flexner, George Washington, Vol. II: *George Washington in the American Revolution, 1775–1783* (Boston: Little, Brown and Co., 1967), p. 324.

81. William B. Willcox, "British Strategy in America, 1778," *Journal of Modern History,* XIX (June 1947), 111.

82. Washington to d'Estaing, July 22, 1778, in Fitzpatrick, ed., *Writings of Washington,* XII, 208.

83. Clinton, *American Rebellion,* p. 100.

84. Mackenzie, *Diary,* I, 309–10.

85. Stephan Popp, *A Hessian Soldier in the American Revolution: The Diary of Stephan Popp,* trans. Reinhart J. Pope (n.p.: privately printed, 1953), p. 11.

86. Washington to Henry Laurens, July 22, 1778, in Fitzpatrick, ed., *Writings of Washington,* XII, 211. Jackson's regiment was one of the sixteen "additional" Continental regiments that were authorized by Congress on December 27, 1776. These regiments were raised "at large." Jackson himself was a native of Massachusetts. See Fred Anderson Berg, *Encyclopedia of Continental Army Units: Battalions, Regiments, and Independent Corps* (Harrisburg: Stackpole Books, 1972), p. 56. As of September 1778, the closest available date to the events in question, Jackson's regiment was carried on the rolls of the Continental Army as having 309 men, of all grades, present and fit for duty. In that same category for the same period, Varnum's brigade is listed as having a total strength of 998. Charles H. Lesser, ed., *The Sinews of Independence: Monthly Strength Reports of the Continental Army* (Chicago: University of Chicago Press, 1976), p. 85. During the month of July, Glover's brigade is placed at a total of 928 present and fit for duty, including all ranks. *Ibid.,* p. 77.

87. Washington to Lafayette, July 22, 1778, in Fitzpatrick, ed., *Writings of Washington,* XII, 202–203.

88. Louis Gottschalk, *Lafayette,* Vol. II: *Lafayette Joins the American Army* (Chicago: University of Chicago Press, 1937), pp. 240–41.

89. Lafayette to Sullivan, July 22, 1778, in Hammond, ed., *Letters and Papers of Sullivan,* II, 101–02.

90. Lafayette to Sullivan, July 22, 1778, in Hammond, ed., *Letters and Papers of Sullivan,* II, 102.

91. Memo, unsigned, concerning Lord Howe's fleet, n.d., Peck MSS Collection, RIHS, V, 64; Thomas L. O'Beirne, *A Candid and Impartial Narrative of the Transactions of the Fleet, under the Command of Lord Howe from the Arrival of the Toulon Squadron, on the Coast of America, to the Time of His Lordship's Departure for England,* 2nd ed. (London: printed for J. Almon, n.d.), pp. 16–17; Charles Stedman, *The History of the Origin, Progress, and Termination of the American War,* 2 vols. (London: J. Murray, J. Debrett, R. J. Kirby, 1794), II, 27; Washington to Henry Laurens, July 22, 1778, in Fitzpatrick, ed., *Writings of Washington,* XII, 210.

92. John Laurens to Henry Laurens, August 4, 1778, in Laurens, *Army Correspondence,* pp. 209–10.

93. Sullivan to Governor Jonathan Trumbull, July 25, 1778, in Hammond, ed., *Letters and Papers of Sullivan,* II, 122.

94. Washington to Sullivan, July 22, 1778, in Fitzpatrick, ed., *Writings of Washington,* XII, 201–02.

95. Nathanael Greene to Sullivan, July 23, 1778, in Hammond, ed., *Letters and Papers of Sullivan,* II, 103.

96. *Ibid.,* p. 104.

97. Charles P. Whittemore, "John Sullivan: Luckless Irishman," in *George Washington's Generals,* ed. George Athan Billias (New York: William Morrow and Co., 1964), p. 139; Whittemore, *A General of the Revolution,* pp. 85–86.

98. Nathanael Greene to Washington, July 23, 1778, in Hammond, ed., *Letters and Papers of Sullivan,* II, 103.

99. Memorandum from Washington to John Laurens, July 22, 1778, in Fitzpatrick, ed., *Writings of Washington,* XII, 206.

100. Washington to John Augustine Washington, in *Ibid.,* p. 488.

101. Henry Marchant to Governor Greene, July 11, 1778, in Staples, *Rhode Island in the Continental Congress,* p. 190.

VI

Delay, Frustration, and a Clever Ruse

ON JULY 27 Washington wrote to Sullivan informing him that he was to have still further aid in the person of Nathanael Greene.[1] In Washington's view, Greene's influence with his fellow Rhode Islanders, his knowledge of the area, his familiarity with the navigation of Narragansett Bay, and his assistance in making preparations by virtue of his position as the Continental Army's quartermaster general would be invaluable.[2] It is also quite possible that a contributing factor in the commander in chief's decision to grant Greene's wish to participate in the expedition was a desire on his part to make a gesture of goodwill toward Greene. Such an action would aid in smoothing a recent misunderstanding between the two generals arising from what Greene saw as Washington's censure of him for a supposed inattentiveness to his advisory role.[3] There can be no doubt that Greene was anxious to go, for in addition to his longing for action, he had not been home in nearly three years.[4]

Leaving army headquarters at White Plains on July 28, Greene arrived at his Coventry iron works by 9:00 P.M. on the 30th.[5] Yet he came only as Sullivan's subordinate. Washington's refusal to appoint either Greene or even the diplomatic Gates, whom Washington saw as his rival, to command the expedition may have been one of the commander in chief's poorest decisions as a soldier. Although Washington maintained military etiquette and retained Sullivan as a political ally by refusing to supersede the mercurial New Hampshireman, Sullivan's past performance had done nothing to justify his retention on a purely military basis.

By way of Greene, Lafayette, whose troops marched into Providence on August 3, received a letter from Washington dated July 27, explaining the necessity of giving the Rhode Islander a command in the expeditionary force in order that his talents might be used to the maximum degree.[6] To that end Washington instructed Sullivan to create two divisions from the ranks of all the American troops—state, militia, and Continentals—including those who had come to Providence with the marquis. One division was to be given to Greene, the other to Lafayette. Justifiably doubtful of the performance of militia, Washington further explained the need for placing Continentals with the irregulars, stating that "the Continental troops being divided in this manner to the Militia, will serve to give them confidence, and probably make them act better than they would alone." [7] Agreeing with Washington as to the necessity of steadying the militia, Lafayette accepted the new arrangement with seeming good grace. To Washington he wrote, "I willingly part with the half of my detachment, though I had a great dependence upon them, as you find it convenient to the good of the service. Any thing, my dear General, you will order, or even wish, shall always be infinitely agreeable to me, and I will always feel happy in doing any thing which may please you, or forward the public good." [8]

While Lafayette and his column marched to Providence and Sullivan continued to carry on the necessary preparations for the coming expedition, John Laurens awaited d'Estaing's squadron at Point Judith with a complement of pilots who had been recruited to guide the fleet through the waters of Narragansett Bay. At the point of rendezvous he bided his time in what he termed "a very disagreeable kind of

MAJOR GENERAL NATHANAEL GREENE

company." [9] The colonel's stay was not to be greatly prolonged, however, for concealed from his eyes by a thick haze, the French fleet anchored off Block Island on the afternoon of July 28. The following morning, as the fog dissipated, Laurens found that the squadron's "appearance was as sudden as a change of decorations in an opera house." [10] By noontime d'Estaing's ships were riding off Point Judith, and Laurens delivered Sullivan's preliminary plan of attack, urging that the three passages of Narragansett Bay be blockaded by the fleet and stressing the necessity of waiting for Lafayette's Continentals before attempting a landing on Rhode Island.[11]

Although d'Estaing had intended to sail up the main channel soon after his arrival and bombard the British batteries guarding Newport's harbor, the day was so far advanced that he was forced to defer a major attack and order his ships to take up blockading stations. By five o'clock on the evening of the 29th the major portion of the French squadron came to anchor off Brenton's Reef, guarding the Middle Channel. At 7:00 P.M. d'Estaing's two smallest frigates, *L'Aimable* and *L'Alcmène,* accompanied by the brigantine *Stanley,* a prize that the French used as a tender, anchored in Seconnet Passage. Shortly after seven o'clock the following morning the fifty-gun *Sagittaire* sealed off Narragansett Passage after running past the British battery at Fox Hill on Conanicut, firing seven or eight shots to the Britons' four. Two hours later Suffern's *Fantasque* (sixty-four guns) entered the channel, and by noon it had joined the *Sagittaire* in Narragansett Passage. Pigot was now completely cut off and alone.[12]

Although Pigot's position was serious, not all was well with the Allies, and the first signs of a strain in relations were beginning to show. Owing to the fact that it was not until July 22 that Sullivan had received news that an attack on Newport was being planned, and that final word had reached him two days later, d'Estaing found upon his arrival that "Sullivan's soldiers are still at home." [13] With a mere 1,600 troops at his disposal as of July 24, and just barely enough provisions to supply them, Sullivan had to gather an army and supplies while d'Estaing was forced to bide time in Narragansett Bay.[14] This was hardly a situation calculated to impress the French admiral with the quality of American military organization, and although his letters to Sullivan were cordial, his private reaction was decidedly negative.[15] Certainly d'Estaing had ample cause to be displeased. As early as July 30 he wrote to Sullivan stating that "the position in which I find myself cannot be ended too soon." [16] After four months at sea scurvy was taking an ever-increasing toll on his men, and by August 4 he had not more than twenty days' rations on hand. Already he had been forced to cut the water allowance.[17] Nor did the Frenchmen's condition measurably improve as the days went by, and they were not overly pleased with the feeble American attempts to supply them.[18] Indeed, d'Estaing seems to have concluded that only with the fall of Newport would he be able to satisfy his needs.[19]

Adding to d'Estaing's anxiety was the inescapable fact that every day the allies waited was another day the enemy gained. Not only was Pigot thus permitted to strengthen his fortifications, but Howe could ready his fleet for an attack, while Clinton was given time to put together a relief force.[20] What must have been even more disconcerting was the knowledge that the British government was sending a fleet across the Atlantic to deal with d'Estaing's squadron—a piece of information that had been in American hands for some time.[21] If this fleet and Howe's combined, d'Estaing's situation would be perilous indeed. Yet Sullivan had no alternative but to wait, and the exertions that he made to prepare his forces freed him from any serious blame for the delay.[22]

Although the American general seems to have slightly overestimated Pigot's strength, placing it at 7,000 men—in fact the British commander had only 6,706 soldiers—and predicting that it would soon grow to 10,000 or 11,000, it is quite possible that Sullivan was not deceived. By asserting a need for a force of 12,000 men and inflating the enemy's numbers, he may well have been making an effort to spur the New England states to turn out a larger number of recruits more rapidly than they might otherwise have done.[23] Still another factor causing Sullivan to look to the creation of a large American army was his fear that events might possibly lead d'Estaing to abandon the expedition, and Sullivan wished to be prepared for any eventuality. This consideration, however, did not itself delay the launching of the allied effort.[24]

Response to Sullivan's call for men varied. On July 29 the Rhode Island Council of War ordered up half of the state's "militia, alarm and independent companies." [25] From Massachusetts came a promise of three thousand troops.[26] Connecticut and New Hampshire were less encouraging. To aid in the reduction of Newport, Connecticut initially ordered the dispatch of a mere seven companies of infantry and one company of matrosses.[27] Only after severe prodding by Sullivan did that state finally vote to raise another five hundred men, making for a promised total force of some fifteen hundred troops under command of the state's Brigadier General John Tyler, a former colonel in the Continental Army.[28] Yet, while Sullivan still found this force inadequate, and despite the backwardness of the state's government, there was still an enthusiasm for the project on the part of Connecticut's people. Ezra Stiles noted that "there is an amazing spirit for rushing toward Rhode Island spread 100 miles round. Militia have gone thither from beyond New Haven." [29]

As for New Hampshire, State Assembly President Weare informed Sullivan that its meager resources of manpower had already been heavily tapped by privateers, the army itself, and Massachusetts, which had hired some five hundred New Hampshiremen to fill her battalions. But Weare promised to try to raise a force despite the treasury's lack of funds to attract volunteers and the fact that there were so few men left. As Weare reported, men were needed

> to Cultivate the land and at this Time of Extreeme drought where the Grass is drying up in the field to secure the Hay which they have just begun to Cutt Especially in the Eastern part of

the State as well as the reaping of the English Corn scarce
leaves a probability of a number being suddenly raised to answer any good end.[30]

As always when relying upon militia, the seasons and the demands of agriculture could often be more formidable than an
enemy army. However, New Hampshire did not desert her native son, and in the early weeks of August some five to six hundred volunteers from that state joined the growing ranks of
Sullivan's army.[31]

Despite the drawbacks in using irregulars, Sullivan had no
other choice, for there was nowhere else to turn. Washington
had sent all the Continentals that could be spared with Lafayette; the rest were needed to watch Clinton's army at New
York, holding at bay a British force that outnumbered
them.[32]

Adding to the imposed delay was the necessity of gathering
boats to transport the expected army and building new ones
to replace those destroyed by Campbell's raiders in their May
attack against Bristol and Warren.[33] To supply his needs,
Sullivan borrowed eleven flat-bottomed boats belonging to
Massachusetts from General Heath, floating them down the
Taunton River at night to the assembly point at Wanton's
Pond near Howland's Ferry in Tiverton.[34]

In order to provide the rest of the needed transports, Sullivan assigned Major Silas Talbot to collect as many boats as
possible and placed him in charge of a company of carpenters
that was to construct eighty-six vessels of the type borrowed
from Heath, each of which was to be capable of carrying one
hundred men.[35]

Twenty-seven years of age, tall in stature and not unhand-
some, Talbot, a resident of Providence and a veteran of the
siege of Boston and Red Bank, set about his task with a zeal
that customarily accompanied his undertakings. Empowered
by Sullivan to seize whatever lumber was required for the
project that could not be purchased, Talbot's men soon completed their assignment.[36] On the day that the construction of
the boats was finished, sixteen of the craft were assembled.

These were caulked that night by candlelight in an open field near Providence, following which the exhausted major made his bed beneath one of the overturned vessels. The next morning the last of the boats were sent on their way to Howland's Ferry.[37]

Essential to the success of the anticipated amphibious operation was the enlistment of experienced men capable of manning the boats gathering at Tiverton. To recruit them Sullivan chose John Glover and issued him the following orders:

> You will please to proceed to Boston, Marblehead and such other places as you may think proper, to engage two or three hundred Seamen or other persons well acquainted with Boats who are to act as Boatmen in the Expedition against Rhode Island.[38]

However, for some unknown reason it appears that Glover never undertook this assignment, for during the period when the boatmen were gathering, Glover remained in Rhode Island. In any case, the seamen turned out in impressive numbers. Marblehead contributed one hundred of them; Salem, twenty-five; Boston, eighty; Newburyport, sixty; and the small coastal towns of both Massachusetts and New Hampshire furnished a few more.[39]

As important as the mustering of troops and the gathering of boats to transport them was the collection of supplies, and in this effort Sullivan spared no energy. So intent was he upon achieving his goal that he empowered his officers to impress supplies that fell under William Heath's jurisdiction—an action that soon brought a rebuke from Heath. Yet, by exercising the diplomacy of which he was capable when so inclined, Heath sought to mend whatever rift may have arisen by attributing Sullivan's move to "Zeal for the Service, and not any design to treat me indelicately." [40] Clearly, Heath held his spleen in check and manifested no direct hostility toward Sullivan. Still, his private sentiments may not have been so charitable, as evidenced by a remark he made during the period when Sullivan began his initial preparations. At that time

Heath grumbled of Sullivan's "raiding" Massachusetts's stores with his constant applications for needed items.[41]

Although Heath could be petty, he could also be cooperative. While his military talents were questionable, his devotion to the Revolution was not, and he did not constitute a serious obstacle to Sullivan's efforts. A graver problem for Sullivan lay elsewhere, for he was forced to send to Washington and the main army at White Plains much of the supplies that he so diligently gathered, a measure that even compelled him to replace his men's standard ration of meat with fish.[42]

Nevertheless, preparations pressed forward and activity proceeded unabated. Even Sunday, a day particularly devoted to the Lord by the fundamentalist tenets of New England, fell victim to the flurry of preparations. On August 2 a local diarist gave the following description of Providence, the site of Sullivan's headquarters:

> This day does not appear like Sunday in this town. All the artificers and tradesmen, with a vast number of persons not belonging to the town, [are] differently employed in preparing with all expedition to go upon the enterprise against the enemy upon Rhode Island.[43]

Much of the burden for equipping the American force and accumulating the needed stores fell upon Captain Asa Waterman, Rhode Island's deputy war commissioner, whose special function as an administrator for the state's Council of War lay in the area of supply. Writing to a friend and fellow supply officer, Waterman lamented that "I . . . have been in such hurry doing every thing that lay in my power ever since the Expedition began I hardly have time to eat drink or sleep." [44] His words are an apt reminder that war is also fought by those who conscientiously toil behind the scenes, and not alone by those who participate in the gore of battle and reap the resulting accolades.

Above all else the Allies needed a workable plan of attack. In it d'Estaing's fleet would, of necessity, play an indispensable role, for without control of the waters of Narragansett

Bay, Sullivan could not send his transports against Rhode Island with any degree of safety, and, if landed, his army would be in danger of being cut off from the mainland and the only route of retreat. Yet, even with d'Estaing present, the invasion force faced a formidable obstacle in Pigot's system of fortifications. These fortifications were composed of three major lines, each of them designed to oppose an attack from the northward, where the ferries constituted the most logical area for an American attack.

The first of these lines, located on the northern portion of the island, consisted of a number of redoubts and lesser works, the most important of which guarded the potential enemy landing places at Bristol Ferry, Commonfence Point, Howland's Ferry, and Fogland Ferry. By far the strongest of the positions was that at Butts Hill,[45] where the British constructed a sizable earthwork, or fortified barrack, designed to be manned by two hundred men. This structure enjoyed a commanding view of the eastern and western sides of Rhode Island, dominated the surrounding countryside, including East and West Main Roads, and formed the center of a fortification system running across the width of the island. In addition to the strongpoints at the extreme north, there were numerous other works, located between Butts Hill and the Middletown-Newport line, which were designed to guard various roads and important geographical features.[46]

Farther to the south, on the heights in back of Newport, lay the two lines that formed the core of Pigot's landward defenses. Occupying advantageous ground and equipped with gates barring the main roads, the outer line first ran from Easton's Pond on the south to the vicinity of Green End on the north. In front of this section of the first line were five redoubts,[47] each of them placed within close proximity to the other, and so located as to cover each other's flanks. Approximately half of the Green End sector was afforded still further protection by Easton's Pond, which lay in the valley between Green End on the west and Honeyman's Hill on the east. In

order to take the maximum advantage of the shelter offered
by the water, the British dammed up the rivulet[48] leading into
the pond from the north, thereby further flooding the marshy
ground above it. Continuing on from Green End, the line then
curved to the northwest, reaching its terminus at the battery
at Coddington Cove, where its flank rested on the bay, secure
from a turning movement by the enemy's infantry. Here, between Green End and the cove, the approaches to the line
were upon flat, relatively open ground, but at the center of the
line, dominating the surrounding countryside, including the
Green End sector, stood Tomini Hill. Rising sharply from the
earth, its rocky northern, eastern, and western slopes were
difficult of ascent even under the best conditions, making it a
natural fortress.[49] To the south the hill gradually descended,
providing a convenient path for the movement of artillery to
the hilltop. There, hollowed from the rock that served to
make the hill so imposing, the British army constructed the
fortification which made Tomini the key to the outer line of
works.

Buttressing the defense of Tomini, which was located just
inside the outer line, and approximately a quarter of a mile in
front of the hill, was a small hillock, Little Tomini. This was
surmounted by a redoubt which, as it stood outside the line of
breastworks, was supported by a small redan.[50]

Behind the first line of the southern intrenchments lay the
second, some three thousand yards in length, at a distance
from the outer line varying from about a quarter of a mile in
the vicinity of Green End to somewhat over a mile in the area
of Tomini Hill. Beginning on the southeast, the line ran from
the area overlooking Easton's Beach and then curved to the
northwest, ending at the North Battery[51] and the bay, thus
forming an arc around the town.[52] Incorporated in this line
were four redoubts, including the North Battery. The redoubt
that anchored the line at its southeastern end commanded the
gap between the two lines at Easton's Beach. Adding to its fire
was a detached redoubt just twenty rods to the north within

the second line. Interspersed between both the inner and outer lines were a number of small works, plus a large detached redoubt that could sweep the fork of East and West Main Roads leading to Newport.[53]

In addition to Pigot's landward defenses were those that guarded the seaward approaches to the town and presented a gauntlet of cannon through which any assailant would have to pass in order to strike at Newport's harbor. The strongest of these works were the Ise Redoubt at Castle Hill, the Prinz Dauneck Redoubt at Brenton's Point (the present site of Fort Adams), and, above all, Fort George,[54] built of stone and heavily intrenched, on Goat Island, just inside the harbor's entrance. Additional batteries covering the water were located at Coddington Cove, Coddington Point, and the North Battery, which also guarded the flank of the inner line of works. Directly across from the Prinz Dauneck Redoubt and Fort George stood a battery mounted at the Dumplings,[55] an odd-shaped rock formation on Conanicut Island. The locations of these last three works formed the points of a triangle, placing any hostile vessel bold enough to venture within it under a triple crossfire from their heavy guns. Also located on Conanicut was the Fox Hill Redoubt at Beaver Head, which guarded the West Passage.[56]

The defenses of the East Passage were not particularly formidable in terms of an in-depth defense. They centered on the redoubts at Fogland Ferry, Howland's Ferry, and Commonfence Point, lying towards the north of Rhode Island. Clearly, the true strength of the British defense lay in the two lines near Newport and the guns pointing at the Middle Passage.[57]

On the southwestern coast of Rhode Island, in the area termed Brenton's Neck, nature protected the British position. There Brenton's Reef and the rocky coastline itself made a landing by small boats, for the purpose of taking the British lines in the rear, hazardous at best.[58] Only in the area stretching from Ochre Point, on the eastern side of the neck, north to Easton's Beach was a landing feasible.[59] Yet, even here the beach was dominated by high hills from which artillery would have a perfect firing position, and the rocky slopes of the "Cliffs" would be difficult to scale. Nowhere would it be possible to assemble assaulting troops in the large formations that the linear tactics of the day demanded. A landing here might become a trap for those men who made it to shore.[60]

To achieve success, Sullivan and d'Estaing had to find a way to smash through or outflank the British defenses. In any such effort the four thousand troops with the French squadron were bound to play a role. The problem was in coordinating their movements and those of the fleet with Sullivan's army.

Before the French fleet's arrival, Sullivan committed to paper his first plan of operations. In a letter to d'Estaing dated July 26, Sullivan suggested that the French commander should move elements of his fleet into the East Passage, where the three British vessels stationed there would be trapped between the French ships and the American batteries at Tiverton Heights. Having disposed of the enemy naval forces there, the French ships could then cover the American landing when the time came. Still other French ships could slip into the West Passage, threatening the two enemy vessels in that area, while the main portion of the French fleet would simultaneously anchor in the Middle Channel, between Conanicut and Rhode Island, cutting off the British in the West Passage from Newport and thus closing the trap. At the same time the British garrison on Conanicut would be isolated and could be dealt with at leisure.

Sullivan proposed that his army should land on the eastern side of the island and then move south to attack the fortifications protecting Newport itself, bypassing the British works on the north. From their ships in the Middle Channel the French troops could make a pretense at landing, giving the Americans an opportunity to reach the island and strike for Newport. The fleet could then land its troops for an attack on the fortifications around the town and bombard the British works on shore. With the fleet in the Middle Channel, possible reinforcements from New York could also be prevented from rendering the garrison aid, and after taking Newport, the Allies could then destroy the enemy forces on the north of the island in the final mop-up operation.[61]

Having stated his ignorance of naval affairs in an effort at diplomacy, Sullivan closed his letter in the same vein, writing apologetically, "please to pardon my Freedom in giving these Hints—Your much superior Judgement will induce You to reject those which You conceive improper & improve on those which You may deem worthy of Notice." [62]

After receiving Sullivan's suggestions from Laurens on July 29, d'Estaing willingly agreed to dispatch part of his force to the East and West Passages. However, an informed judgment led him to abandon his original design of forcing his way into the Main Channel. Although his decision apparently surprised many of his officers, the admiral's pilots had warned him that it would be impossible to anchor his squadron anywhere but within range of the triangular crossfire of the enemy batteries at Brenton's Point, Goat Island, and the Dumplings. Due to the danger of contrary winds that might not allow him to turn the north point of Conanicut at will, and the narrowness of the Middle Channel at its northern end, a movement by the main segment of d'Estaing's squadron up the West Passage with the design of rounding the northern end of Conanicut, and then sailing down the Main Passage, seemed out of the question. As a result, in the gentlest terms possible, d'Estaing rejected this part of Sullivan's plan, and on July 30 he sent Laurens and Colonel Fleury, who had sailed with the fleet from Sandy Hook, to Sullivan with a counter-proposal. For his part, d'Estaing requested that Sullivan send a portion of his militia to assist the French in capturing Conanicut, thus silencing its menacing guns and snaring its garrison.[63]

While en route to deliver d'Estaing's message, the two intermediaries received word that American privateers had

landed on Conanicut and found the Fox Hill Battery abandoned. Shortly thereafter they encountered Sullivan himself,
who, eager to meet his new colleague and discuss some
changes in his original plan,[64] was on his way to the squadron,
and they relayed the French admiral's request. Upon his arrival Sullivan was greeted with the proper show of cordiality;
in Laurens's words, the general was "received on board with
the guard of marines, and the drums beating to arms; and, at
his departure, the ship was manned and fifteen cannon
fired." [65] Yet the problem of how to deal with Conanicut remained unresolved in the minds of the Allied commanders.[66]

While his enemies delayed their attack pending the arrival
of Sullivan's army and tried to hammer out a plan on which
they could agree, Pigot made good use of the delay. Yet his
efforts were made against a background of demoralizaton on
the part of the Tory population, and at least a part of his
army. With the sighting of the French on the morning of July
29, the town was thrown into confusion and despair.[67] Such
was the despondency that Captain Mackenzie noted on August 2:

> Few or none of the Inhabitants have offered their services for
> the defense of the Garrison: even those who associated last win-
> ter for that purpose,[68] are now so alarmed, and many of them so
> certain that the place will be reduced, that they have declined
> acting at all in The King's Service. A few of the Merchants who
> came here with The Army, and one or two young Gentlemen of
> the place, have desired to serve as Volunteers with some of the
> Regiments.[69]

Among the troops, perhaps those who were most depressed
were the Hessians,[70] one of whom wrote that "We supposed as
a matter of course that we should be taken prisoners. . . ." [71]
This state of mind soon became known to the Americans due
to the numerous deserters, British as well as Hessian, who
made their way into the rebel lines, bringing with them information regarding the British dispositions.[72]

As for Pigot, if he felt any undue anxiety at this stage, he refused to show it. Soon after the appearance of the French fleet he hurried a dispatch boat on its way to British head-quarters at New York with word of d'Estaing's arrival, and throughout the early period of the crisis boats slipped out nearly every night for New York to keep Clinton informed of the course of events.[73]

From the tone of Pigot's letters, Clinton concluded that "he writes perfectly cool and quiet and does not seem to be under the least apprehension."[74] Indeed, his determination to de-fend his post to the last seemed inflexible, for he announced that should the enemy take Newport, he intended to burn the town in order to drive them out and maintain his hold on the ground.[75]

In preparation for the impending siege, Pigot determined to withdraw the troops from the north end of the island and place them inside the lines surrounding Newport once the French fleet attempted to force its way into the harbor. Thus the enemy would be prevented from cutting his army in two.[76] Similarly, on July 29, fearing the isolation of his men on Con-anicut, Pigot withdrew Brown's Provincial Regiment and the two Anspach battalions stationed there, leaving only two small detachments, some fifty men in all, to man the guns at the Dumplings and Fox Hill. The following day, after two ships of the line from d'Estaing's squadron had run past the battery at Fox Hill, the same fear that had moved Pigot on the 29th led him to recall the remaining men. As there were not enough oxen to haul away the guns, those at Fox Hill were spiked and the magazine was exploded, while the two twenty-four-pounders at the Dumplings were hurled down the rocks into the sea.[77] Unbeknown to them, Pigot had solved for the Allies their difference over how to deal with Conanicut.

Throughout the long preinvasion period, Pigot drove his men. When the island's Black population refused to respond in large numbers to a call to join the British army with the promise of pay and provisions, the troops gathered them up and compelled them to enter inside the southern defenses, where their services were needed as drivers and laborers.[78] In addition, the prisoners who had been removed from the prison ships and sent to Portsmouth when the French appeared were marched to Newport.[79]

As a preliminary to the concentration of his forces around Newport, by August 4 Pigot had withdrawn his stores and all his guns from the north of the island, with the exception of a twelve-pounder at the Bristol Ferry Redoubt and a nine-pounder at Howland's Point, both potential American landing places. Thus his troops could retreat to the south unencumbered when the time came.[80]

Carriages, carts, and wagons, as well as wheelbarrows, pick-axes, shovels, and all manner of intrenching tools, were gathered up and sent to the defenses of Newport, while the island's cattle and horses were also driven within the lines. As an added precaution, Pigot issued an order to disarm the island's inhabitants.[81]

Yet, amid the rush of his martial preparations and with his threat to burn the town if necessary, the British commander did not show himself devoid of humanity. In gathering the livestock, Pigot took care that the families thus deprived were allowed to keep one of their cows for their own subsistence. Still further, although willing to destroy those buildings which were in range of his perimeter and provided cover for an approaching enemy, Pigot rejected a proposal to burn all the houses on the island that stood outside his lines. Militarily such a measure could avail him nothing, for in the middle of summer the lack of shelter from the elements was not deemed a serious inconvenience to the enemy, and it could only produce suffering on the part of the innocent.[82] In Mackenzie's words, such a deed would "cause a stain upon our arms." [83]

All the while the fortifications grew in strength, and new works were added.[84] The men were continually engaged in constructing abatis around the redoubts of the southern defenses and clearing away any obstructions in their front that could shelter the enemy. From Green End to Tomini Hill, an entire line of abatis was placed in front of the outer line. In order to deal with any possible threat to his rear, Pigot raised two small redoubts, complete with cannon, on the high ground commanding the road from Brenton's Neck to Newport, thus adding to the natural obstacles that protected him in that area.[85]

Advantage was taken of the summer's heat, and thirst became an ally when the British filled in the wells of Portsmouth. To further hamper the Americans, trees were felled across the roads in Portsmouth and Middletown to obstruct their line of march.[86]

As for the French fleet, Pigot also sought to create a barrier that would hinder its maneuvers. Accordingly, Captain Ralph Brisbaine, commander of the British naval forces at Newport, acting under Pigot's orders, busied his men in stripping the prison ships and transports and prepared them for scuttling in order to block up the harbor. On August 3 six of them were sunk along a line stretching from the north end of Goat Island to the North Battery, making it impossible for the enemy to approach nearer than a point eight hundred yards from the batteries in that area. Two days later four more of the hulks were sent to the bottom on the west side of Goat Island, obstructing the harbor's southern entrance. The stumps of their masts, cut off seven feet from their decks, rose just above the water's surface, a warning for the French to keep off. None of this went unnoticed by d'Estaing, who was given another cause to regret the delay in the Allied operations.[87]

Forming a barrier in the harbor was not the whole extent of Pigot's naval concerns. Fearing that the vessels of Newport's small naval squadron might be captured, as early as July 29 he instructed Brisbaine that under no circumstances were the ships to be allowed to fall into enemy hands.[88]

As a result of Pigot's order, July 30 saw the first acts of heroism performed during the siege. At one o'clock that afternoon, the frigates *L'Aimable* and *L'Alcmène,* with the brigantine *Stanley,* which had entered the East Passage on the evening of the 29th, got under way and moved to attack the three British ships trapped in the channel. To assist in the attack, the senior French officer had solicited the aid of a number of American fieldpieces that were to prevent the British galleys from seeking the shelter of the shoal waters of the Tiverton side of the passage. As soon as the French reached Black Point, nearly a mile and a half from where the eighteen-gun British sloop *King's Fisher* and the galleys *Alarm* and *Spitfire* were riding at anchor under the shelter of the Fogland Redoubt, the *King's Fisher* was set afire, while the galleys ran nearly a half mile up the channel to Sandy Point. There they too were put to the torch by their crews.

While the three vessels blazed into flames, their fully shotted guns firing as the heat reached them, the French shortened sail and halted off Black Point, cannonading the dying English ships. With their maneuverability restricted by the narrow channel, the French ships now became perfect targets for the flaming vessels. Thus, with her sails set, the abandoned *Spitfire* was directed on a course towards the French force. In a desperate effort to avert the threatened collision, the Count de Grasse-Limermont put out with a crew in a longboat. Grappling the floating inferno, he towed it clear, just as the fire reached the *Spitfire's* magazine. Shaken but unhurt, the intrepid Frenchmen had accomplished their goal.

After burning almost to the water's edge, the *King's Fisher* broke free of her anchor and drifted down past Fogland Point. In a forlorn attempt to save her, a group of sailors under M. de Dorset boarded the sloop from their boats and made a valiant effort to extinguish the flames, while the burning ship drifted toward the mainland and grounded. Suddenly her powder room exploded, but luck was with de Dorset and his men, who escaped unscathed.[89] Now nothing save the redoubts on the north blocked Sullivan's landing.[90]

The demise of Brisbaine's ships in the East Passage was soon followed by that of another portion of his squadron. Due to a misreading of the intentions of the French frigates in the West Passage, the British concluded that both the *Sagittaire* and the *Fantasque* were planning to abandon the channel and rejoin the main fleet. As a result, the four British vessels which had run down towards Newport on August 2 were ordered to resume their former stations on the western side of Rhode Island in order to cut off communication by water between the Narragansett shore and Bristol Neck, as well as to prevent American privateers from landing on the island. Accordingly, the *Pigot Galley* and the frigate *Lark* dropped anchor opposite Prudence Island between Coggeshall and Arnold's Points. The frigate *Orpheus* rode off the north end of Dyer's Island, and the frigate *Cerberus* anchored to the south of Dyer's.

At five o'clock on the morning of August 5, the *Sagittaire* and the *Fantasque,* plus a third two-decker which had joined them in the West Passage the day before, got under way and rounded the northern tip of Conanicut. Seeing her danger, the *Cerberus* slipped her cable and attempted to run for Newport. As the French drew nearer, Captain Symmons realized he would be cut off and ran his ship aground on the shores of Rhode Island. While one of the French frigates vainly bombarded them, Symmons brought his crew safely to shore and set his ship aflame. By 8:00 A.M. she exploded.

Tacking her sails, the French vessel that had fired on Symmons made for Coddington's Cove, causing the frigate *Juno* to be put to the torch. Remaining on course, the French ship opened fire on the battery at Coddington's Cove, where the panic-stricken sailors manning the redoubt spiked their guns and ran for their lives.

To the north, their escape now impossible, and with two French warships bearing down on them, the *Orpheus, Lark,* and *Pigot Galley* were run ashore and set afire. The *Orpheus* exploded at seven o'clock, throwing debris for three miles. At noon the *Pigot Galley* blew up, and the *Lark,* loaded with seventy-six barrels of powder, erupted with a thunderous roar, consuming a nearby house in flames.

Their enemies destroyed, the French vessels put about and calmly anchored off the north point of Conanicut at 9:00 A.M.[91]

Even with most of their warships gone, the garrison's naval problems were not yet at an end. The shores of Rhode Island now lay open to the American privateers which had already been harrying Conanicut. Soon their crews began descending on the western shore of Rhode Island, pillaging, destroying,[92] and, as Captain Mackenzie euphemistically put it, "beating and ill-treating the Women." [93] Whether they scrupled to make a distinction between Whig and Tory remains an open question.

The misery of the civilian population in Newport was further compounded by the now shipless sailors who formerly had guarded the community. As Mrs. Mary Almy, whose Whiggish husband had deserted her to join the American army, recorded in her journal on August 5 following the burning of the ships in the Main Channel:

> At night they ordered all the sailors into town, if possible to keep some order with them. Never was there a more curious sight. . . . Every sailor was equipt with a musket that could get one; he that could not, had a billet of wood, an old broom, or any club they could find. They all took care to save a bottle of spirits, which they call *kill grief*; some fiddling, some playing on jewsharps, all in high spirits, though they had not a second shirt. . . . By dark the bottles were exhausted, and they so unruly that we were obliged to be safely housed that night.[94]

To maintain order among the "tars" and strengthen his defenses, Pigot had the sailors formed into a corps commanded by the garrison's naval officers and assigned them to man the guns of his batteries. In forming an encampment for these unruly warriors, he also took care to place it outside the inner line and away from the town.[95]

Morale took a decided upturn on August 3, when at 4:00 A.M. two small tenders from New York ran through the French fleet under cover of a heavy fog and headed for Rhode Island. One landed safely, while the other was fired on and pursued by small boats from the French warships. Keeping a cool hold on himself and his men, her captain ran the little vessel ashore at Castle Hill, on Brenton's Neck, and, as the Frenchmen drew near, ordered his men to open fire. The resulting volley from the Britishers' small arms and swivel guns ripped into their enemies, hitting some of them and causing them to draw off. Safely ashore, the two officers delivered the dispatches they carried from Clinton and Admiral Howe, dated July 30 and 31, promising immediate assistance. Indeed, the two men informed the garrison that Howe was already on his way. Having been joined by three more ships, one of them from Byron's fleet, Howe deemed himself strong enough to sally forth against the French, and the officers had seen him moving his fleet out from Sandy Hook on the last day of July. Now relief was in the offing and Pigot needed only to hold out.[96]

While Pigot prepared his men for the coming battle and awaited the relief expedition, the Allies continued to thrash out a plan of attack. Following the British evacuation of Conanicut on July 30 and the arrival of news of this move from the American privateers operating near the island, d'Estaing sent a scouting party ashore in the evening to determine whether the rumor was accurate. Finding the enemy gone, the French hoisted their flag and took possession.[97] The first major obstacle to Allied cooperation was removed, but it was soon to be followed by others even more formidable.

With the problem of dealing with Conanicut out of the way, d'Estaing and Sullivan finally agreed upon a plan of operations, and by August 3 they were looking forward to the setting of a day for the assault to begin, probably none more eagerly than the anxious d'Estaing. In its essentials it was the same scheme formulated by Sullivan in his letter of July 25. As before, Sullivan's men were to land on the east side of Rhode Island, under cover from the fire of three French frigates in the East Passage, bypassing the British line centered on Butts Hill. On a signal from the Americans, the French were then to come ashore on the west and the two forces were to link up as quickly as possible.[98] Simple and direct as it was, the plan ran into difficulty almost immediately.

What Nathanael Greene termed Lafayette's "great thirst for glory and national attachment" [99] combined to set Allied relations upon a basis of something less than complete amiability. Lafayette, who had defied his king to come to America and aid its cause, became the primary catalyst for the first real clash of Allied national and personal sensibilities. Following d'Estaing's proposal that the young marquis lead the French forces at Newport, Lafayette had become obsessed with the idea of being the first to combine French and American troops under a single command.[100] This plume Lafayette hoped to add to an easy victory and its attendant applause. As he expressed his sentiments to Sullivan, "I hope a pretty decent crop of laurels may be collected upon that island, and we will terminate the whole by joining English *country dances* to French cotillions in company with the fine and reputed ladies of that charming place." [101]

Soon after his arrival in Providence on August 2, a day ahead of his men who encamped twelve miles outside of town, Lafayette paid an informal visit to the French fleet.[102] On August 4 Sullivan asked the young Frenchman to call upon d'Estaing once again. This time Lafayette was to go for the purpose of arranging some of the few remaining details which had been omitted from the plan of operations, a plan that did not envision the creation of the joint Franco-American command for which Lafayette so eagerly longed. At 9:00 A.M. Lafayette and a number of French and American officers came aboard the *Languedoc*. During the course of his discussion with the admiral, the marquis allowed ambition to get the better of him, and he urged d'Estaing to write to Sullivan and press for a combination of Lafayette's Continentals and the French troops on board the fleet. By five o'clock that evening Lafayette and his entourage departed, sailing for Providence on board one of d'Estaing's ships, the *Provence*.[103]

That same day d'Estaing complied with Lafayette's plea
and included the proposed change in plan in a missive that
dealt with a number of other problems as well. Requesting
that the attack by the two Allied forces be made simultaneously and that two diversionary assaults be launched to divide the British garrison, d'Estaing's reasoning was not without merit, particularly from the standpoint of a man who had
to care for a fleet as well as a landing force. He wrote:

> The Marquis de la Fayette will describe to you the peril in
> which we should find ourselves if I were obliged to reëmbark to
> resist a maritime enemy.[104] This purpose, and that of dividing
> the forces of the English by presenting to them a more imposing
> front than we could otherwise do, make me desire that you
> might deem it suitable that a wing or at least a portion of your
> army should attack at the same time and in the same place as
> our men. You would be still more certain that all would act at
> the same instant. Should your choice fall then on Monsieur the
> Marquis de la Fayette the unity of the movement would be as-
> sured; he would always command your troops and he would
> find himself in my absence naturally at the head of the
> French.[105]

When Lafayette reported the results of his mission to Sullivan the following morning,[106] he continued to press his cause
and, according to Laurens, "strenuously contended that a
considerable detachment of select troops ought to be annexed
to the French. The pride of his nation would never suffer the
present disposition to take place, as by it the French batal-
lions w^d land under cover of the American fire, and play a
humiliating secondary part." [107] Now national jealousy was
openly making its appearance on the scene.

In responding to Lafayette's application, Sullivan reasoned
that, as d'Estaing would very likely accompany his men and
retain command of them, Lafayette would be more useful if
he remained with the American army and continued to lead
its left wing. Even more important, both Sullivan and Greene
felt that the army consisted of far too few regulars as it was
and that a detachment of any of them would risk a disaster

From E. A. Duyckinck, *National Portrait Gallery of Eminent Americans*, I, 315

MARQUIS DE LAFAYETTE

should any hard fighting occur. The Continentals were the heart of the American offensive and the shield of the rest of Sullivan's troops, for raw militia were notorious for their tendency to panic in a crisis.[108]

Lafayette remained dissatisfied, and Laurens accurately perceived that his colleague's "private views withdrew his attention wholly from the general interest." [109] Petulantly the marquis wrote to d'Estaing in a letter that clearly reveals his state of mind:

> I know that it is not pleasant for some people to watch the best scenes in a play taken by foreign actors. I believe that the French will somewhat eclipse their neighbors and that the best dramatic efforts will probably fall to their lot. General Sullivan's attack, although very important, would be somewhat like what they call on the stage a rehearsal *en robe de chambre,* compared with the spectacle which your fleet and troops would present. I confess that I would not like to see French troops among people whose foreign hearts would not appreciate their value.[110]

Lafayette then went on to urge that d'Estaing persevere in his request for a change in plan and that two thousand American troops, from one-half to at least one-third of them regulars, be assigned to act in conjunction with the French landing force. The marquis also assured him that a firm stance on the subject would place the American generals in a position where they would "find it easier to submit than answer you." [111] In concluding, Lafayette entreated the admiral to ask that the young Frenchman be offered command of such a contingent.[112]

At first d'Estaing's response to Lafayette's suggestion was the adoption of a policy of conciliation and moderation. On August 6 he wrote to Sullivan stating his willingness to acquiesce in the American's design. At the same time the admiral tried to absolve Lafayette of the blame which Sullivan placed on him for the disagreement that had arisen, making the noble gesture of taking it on himself; "I find only that you pun-

ish M. le Mis de la Fayette a little too much for a mistake that
is mine," d'Estaing wrote.[113]

With the attack set for Sunday, August 9, d'Estaing also
tried to soothe the injured feelings of Lafayette, urging him to
resign himself to his disappointment for the sake of the common good.[114] Yet, that same day Lafayette was writing to his
mentor, Washington:

> The Admiral wants me to join the French troops to those I
> command, as soon as possible. I confess I feel very happy to
> think of my coöperating with them; and, had I continued in my
> mind an agreeable dream, I could not have wished a more pleas-
> ing event than my joining my countrymen with my brothers of
> America, under my command, and the same standards.[115]

There was no mollifying him.

August 7 saw d'Estaing return to his previous insistence
that his troops and Sullivan's land simultaneously, and that
an American contingent cooperate with him. His words in-
voked the spirit of the alliance and, however politely framed,
left no doubt as to his meaning:

> I dare hope that Your Excellency and the General Officers who
> serve with you, will put it in my power to give an account to the
> King and to the Congress of the Number and goodness of the
> troops that you shall have joined to the French—This detach-
> ment the number of which I will not undertake to point out be-
> cause on all occasions we endeavour when it is necessary to be
> sufficient to themselves—is the first occasion on which the Gen-
> erals of the United States have it in their power to give an au-
> thentic proof of the value which they set upon the alliance of
> His Majesty and the satisfaction with which they join their
> troops to his. . . .[116]

With his own troops and the Americans which he called for,
d'Estaing promised that he would move towards Sullivan and
"effect our union." [117]

There was little that Sullivan could do, for d'Estaing's cooperation was essential to the expedition's success and much
was expected of the first Allied effort. Thus he accepted the

counsel that Washington had given him earlier concerning what might be termed "military diplomacy." [118] In regard to the leadership of the French troops, Washington had wisely cautioned the New Hampshireman that d'Estaing's "wish should be complied with, as to the particular of them. I should suppose the Marquis would be his choice." [119] As for Sullivan's relations with the admiral, the commander in chief had realistically advised that "harmony and the best understanding between us should be a Capital and first object. The Count himself is a Land Officer of the high rank of Lt. General in the French Army." [120]

For the good of the expedition, Sullivan relented and promised to give to Lafayette Colonel Henry Jackson's regiment of Continentals and as many militiamen as would raise the total number of troops in the force to one thousand men. At the same time, Sullivan deferred the attack until daybreak on August 10, giving himself still another day to complete the construction of his transports and allow the heavy cannon and more militia to arrive.[121]

Although the marquis grumbled at the small size of the contingent, he accepted the offer which he and d'Estaing had succeeded in extorting from the American general;[122] and while Sullivan chose to delay still longer, d'Estaing elected to adhere to his original timetable and force the Middle Channel on August 8.[123]

On the morning of the 8th, at eleven o'clock, leaving the seventy-four gun *Protecteur* to guard the entrance of the Middle Channel, eight of the French ships of the line which had been standing off Brenton's Reef got under way. With the wind blowing from the south-southwest, they tacked to the east, towards the West Passage. Then, with room to maneuver before the wind, they stood for the Middle Channel in two parallel lines, with d'Estaing and the eighty-gun *Languedoc* in the lead. At 3:00 P.M. the first ships came within range of the fourteen guns at Brenton's Point, Goat Island, and the North Battery, manned by seamen from the British frigates that had been destroyed. As panicked civilians who had come to watch the spectacle fled wildly through the streets of the town, the ships' guns blasted at the enemy emplacements, which in turn spewed forth an eruption of fire and smoke in reception. For an hour and a quarter the cannonade continued, the French firing inaccurately, with most of their shots passing over the town, landing near the encampment of one of the Anspach regiments, and the British scoring numerous hits, one of them cutting away the admiral's colors. Hugging the Conanicut shore, for the sunken transports near Goat Island and a third line of them stretching from the North Battery to Rose Island would allow the French to come no closer to the batteries, the ships escaped serious damage. At five o'clock they anchored safely beyond range of the British guns in a line between Conanicut and Gold islands.[124]

While the French ran past the batteries, Commodore Brisbaine completed the task of disposing of his squadron, scuttling the sloop *Faulcon* off the southeastern end of Goat Island and the frigate *Flora* between the island and Long Wharf. The rest of the transports were also sent to the bottom, with the sole exception of the *Grand Duke of Russia,* a former East Indiaman, which was run ashore between Goat Island and the North Battery. There, not more than twenty yards from the docks and nearby provision-laden storehouses, she was set afire and became a burning torch that spread its flames to the storehouses and a number of nearby dwellings. Though the fires on shore were quickly extinguished, firefighting parties from the army were forced to work until midnight.[125]

Soon after the French dropped anchor, Pigot gave orders to burn all buildings within range of the guns in the redoubts of the outer line, and about twenty were put to the torch. At four o'clock the British commander also instructed his officers to withdraw the troops from the northern part of the island. Shortly after 8:00 P.M. they marched within the lines about Newport. Now Pigot's entire force of 6,706 men was concentrated in a strong defensive position, ready for the blow that its leader knew must soon come.[126]

On Sunday, August 9, Sullivan wrote once again to d'Estaing, reiterating his intention to make his assault on Monday.[127] In the interim Sullivan proposed to drill his men in the procedure of embarking and reembarking with their boats.[128] Most important of all, in the case of what he termed "the Motley and dissaranged Chaos of Militia," the delay would give him an opportunity for "arranging with more precision, the dismberd Parts of this unwieldy Body—if any Power less than the Almighty fiat, coud reduct them to order." [129]

Shortly after sending his message to the admiral, Sullivan learned of Pigot's evacuation of the northern forts by way of some deserters from Pigot's army, whose testimony was verified by separate intelligence from some of the island's inhabitants. Fearful lest the British commander reverse his move and reoccupy the works, Sullivan called a council of war during which his officers concurred with his decision to immediately land a force under Colonel John Topham to hold the redoubts and then cross with the rest of the army. Sullivan next dispatched an officer to d'Estaing with word of his action and a request that the French join his troops.[130]

A 8:00 A.M. the bulk of the American troops began crossing Howland's Ferry from their headquarters at Fort Barton and headed for Butts Hill.[131] There some of the eager and inexperienced militiamen expected a fight. In the disappointed words of Private Noah Robinson, a young farm boy from Marlborough, Massachusetts, he and his fellows "Formed and Marched Boldly up to the Fourt, on the N. End of ye Island, then Was Informed ye Enemy had Retreated to the South End of ye Island." [132]

Much to his surprise, d'Estaing received Sullivan's message concerning the landing only an hour after the arrival of the American general's letter promising to attack the next day. Although d'Estaing later expressed approval and even praised Sullivan for his response to changing circumstances, the im-

mediate reaction of the French was hardly a positive one.[133]
John Laurens reported that "this measure gave much um-
brage to the French officers. They conceived their troops injured by our landing first, and talked like women disputing
precedence in a country dance, instead of men engaged in pursuing the common interest of two great nations." [134]

Nevertheless, having been informed that Sullivan had only
some two thousand men on the island at the moment,
d'Estaing prepared to land his men and come to the Americans' aid.[135] In addition to debarking his four thousand
troops, d'Estaing also proposed to strip his ships of their crews
in order to swell the numbers of his force to ten thousand, an
idea not universally popular with his officers. From their
standpoint, the absence of the crews from their vessels exposed the ships needlessly, for the seamen could be of little use
on the island. As one of the officers put it, "such a force is fit
for nothing for pillaging; without discipline, it occasions disorder." [136] A disorder of another kind was soon to put an end to
all of d'Estaing's plans.

Leaving orders for his men to follow him to Conanicut,
where they could be formed for the attack, the admiral hurried ashore to confer with Sullivan. Enroute, d'Estaing received a disquieting jolt, for as the morning fog cleared away
at noon, it revealed a fleet, which d'Estaing placed at thirty-
six sail, standing off the bay.[137] Howe had arrived.

On Rhode Island, troops and civilians alike, including General Prescott, flocked to Brenton's Neck to get a view of their
saviors.[138] They expected to see the destruction of the French
fleet, and, in Captain Mackenzie's words, "the spirits of the
whole Garrison were at this period elevated to the highest
pitch." [139] Perhaps those whose elation was the most openly
displayed were the sailors whose "joy was so great as to tear
all their tents, and play fury with everything in their
reach." [140]

At three o'clock the *Guerrier,* which had approached
Howe's fleet to confirm its identity, signaled d'Estaing's ships
that the newly arrived force was indeed an enemy. Immedi-

ately orders were issued to return the men who were on the way to Conanicut to the fleet, and for reembarking the scurvy-stricken sailors who had been sent ashore for relief after the forcing of the channel. Then, with the landing parties back on board and signal flags fluttering from the masts of the *Languedoc,* the French ships ranged themselves broadside across the channel, preparing to rake Howe's ships if he attempted to enter.[141]

Wisely Howe chose to remain outside the channel, and at 6:00 P.M. his ships dropped anchor between Point Judith and the lighthouse at Beaver Tail.[142]

At one o'clock that afternoon, while the main portion of Howe's fleet was still in motion, Pigot and Brisbaine had dispatched three of their officers in two small boats to the frigates that Howe had sent ahead to Brenton's Neck to open communications with Newport. Their mission was to give the admiral an account of their situation and learn how the garrison could cooperate with his expected attack. Later that evening some of the sailors from Brisbaine's command were sent out to the fleet to help man Howe's warships.[143]

What Howe could do was problematical. On July 25 he had been reinforced by the *Renown* (50 guns), which had arrived from the West Indies. July 30 saw the arrival of the *Cornwall* (74 guns), one of Byron's ships, which brought the welcome news that his storm-battered fleet was heading for New York. The next day Howe was joined by the *Raissonable* (64 guns) and *Centurion* (50 guns) from Halifax. Strengthened by these reinforcements and unwilling to be encumbered by transports at a time when speed was essential, Howe sailed from Sandy Hook on August 6 after being delayed by contrary winds. With him he had eight ships of the line, twelve frigates, three fire ships, two bomb ketches, three small ships, and four galleys. Yet the French had the greater weight of metal, some 846 pieces to Howe's 772. Meanwhile, Clinton continued to prepare a relief force of four thousand men.[144]

Although Howe had publicly stated that he intended to

LORD RICHARD HOWE

attack the French, those closest to him believed that he intended to try to lure d'Estaing away from the siege and attempt to postpone any naval action until Byron could join
him, as he later asserted.[145] Accordingly, Howe chose to defer
his attack, a course of action approved by his subordinates, for
the French held a position from which they could be assisted
by guns that the Americans were believed to have placed on
the north end of Conanicut. Thus it seemed impossible to
afford Pigot any immediate material relief—all Howe could do
was wait.[146] The next move was up to the French.

    D'Estaing and his commanders took quite a different view
of the situation than did Howe, and theirs was equally realistic. Their force was badly divided for the purpose of meeting a
naval foe. Two of the French ships were out on patrol, three
more were in the East Passage, two were at the northern tip of
Conanicut, and the remaining eight ships of the line were
astride the Main Channel. While the vessels in the bay might
be joined, with some difficulty in the case of those to the east,
the French position was potentially weak in other ways as
well. Knowing that Howe had some troops with him,[147]
d'Estaing feared that if he remained in the Main Channel
Howe might occupy Conanicut, establish batteries, and place
the French in a crossfire between that island and the guns at
Newport. Moreover, if Howe attacked d'Estaing in the bay,
Howe's ships would be more maneuverable than d'Estaing's
larger ones, and the fire ships and bomb ketches would give
the British a decided advantage. Neither could d'Estaing
afford to allow himself to be blockaded in the harbor, for then
he could not provide protection to the valuable French possessions in the West Indies, a major part of his mission. Above
all, if Byron joined Howe, as the French expected would hap-
pen, the British would have overpowering naval superiority.
Howe had to be crushed before the juncture could take
place.[148] Accordingly, following a conference of his captains
on the night of August 9, d'Estaing notified Sullivan of his determination to defeat Howe on the open sea and then return
to continue the siege.[149]

Writing late on the evening of the 9th, Sullivan stated his disbelief that Howe could have arrived and urged d'Estaing to remain and complete the capture of Newport. Assuring the admiral that his fleet was in no danger, Sullivan sought to allay d'Estaing's fears by telling him that his ships could be covered against any attack by the redoubts that the Americans had occupied on the north end of Rhode Island. Carefully Sullivan avoided any mention of the fact that the redoubts as yet had no guns in them.[150]

Sullivan's message reached d'Estaing on August 10, just as his ships began to move out to sea. Having begun his movement, the French admiral chose to let his actions be his reply.[151] Whatever his feelings may have been at the time, his chagrin at the failure of the Americans to detect Howe's move from New York to Rhode Island was later bitterly expressed to Congress:

> However unexpected, surprising, and miraculous General Sullivan found the appearance of this fleet, as he did me the honor to inform me in his letter . . . , its existence was not the less certain. Nothing had announced it to me; not the least intelligence of the dispositions and departure of the English had reached me; the surprise was complete.[152]

It was not until August 8, two days after Howe had sailed, that Washington sent word of the fleet's departure from Sandy Hook. Although he correctly gauged Howe's action as an attempt to draw the French away from Rhode Island and not to do battle, the commander in chief's letter arrived too late to do any good.[153]

Ordering three frigates and a brigantine to remain in the East Passage to protect Sullivan's communications with the mainland, d'Estaing prepared to give battle. The two ships at the north end of Conanicut had joined him in the Main Channel, and he awaited only a favorable wind.[154]

On August 10 the wind shifted to the northeast, giving d'Estaing the weather gauge and enabling him to drive down the channel towards Howe. At 7:00 A.M. d'Estaing hoisted the signal to begin the movement and, cutting their cables, the ten ships got under way. Just before 8:30 the French, steering along the coast of Conanicut to avoid the British guns, came within range of Pigot's batteries, and once again they thundered at one another. For an hour and a quarter the exchange went on. While the British guns frequently found their targets despite the great range, most of the fleet's shots soared over the emplacements, plunging into the town and striking houses but miraculously wounding no one. The British emerged from the contest unscathed, but the effect of their fire was pointed up by the French dead who were washed up on the beaches of Rhode Island.[155] Once past the batteries the ten French warships were joined by the *Protecteur* (74 guns), which sailed out of the West Passage,[156] and "they crouded all the sail they could set, even to Studding Sails and Royals, and stood directly for the British fleet." [157]

For Howe to give battle he would have to tack against the wind, and the fire ships, in which he placed such great faith to offset d'Estaing's superior firepower, would be useless. With this additional reason for refusing combat, he bore away on a course heading south-southeast, with the wind and the French at his back. All that day the two fleets maneuvered for position, maintaining contact through the night.[158]

On the morning of the second day, amid thickening weather and with the two fleets some eight miles apart, Howe, sensing a growing restlessness for action among the men, began to execute a carefully planned movement designed to gain the weather gauge. At eight o'clock he turned his line of battle from the southeast to the south. Foolishly d'Estaing continued to press after the sternmost of Howe's fleet, rather than holding his wind advantage. At 11:30 A.M. Howe shifted to the west, and at 1:30 to the northwest. Shortly after four o'clock he had nearly weathered d'Estaing and was preparing to spring upon him when the French fleet began to bear away to the south. In the increasingly heavy seas d'Estaing's ships were soon lost from sight. Towards sunset the threatening weather turned into a violent gale, which continued until the afternoon of August 13 and scattered both fleets.[159]

At dusk on the evening of the 13th d'Estaing's *Languedoc,* alone and dismasted, her rudder broken, was attacked by the *Renown* under Captain Dawson. Blasting the crippled Frenchman with three broadsides, the *Renown* shot away her rudder, killed sixty officers and men, and wounded as many more. Then, with darkness closing in, Dawson drew off to await the morning and the completion of his work. The new day saw d'Estaing saved from his plight as six French ships came into sight. Discovering the *Renown* and another vessel that was closing for an attack, three of them vainly gave chase while the others stood guard over the *Languedoc.* At 9:00 A.M. that portion of the fleet which had rejoined the flagship rescued the *Marseilles* (which had lost her foremast and bowsprit in the storm) from another Britisher. During the evening of the 13th the *Marseilles* had been engaged by Commodore Hotham of the *Preston,* who then hove to, planning to recommence his assault on the 14th. Frustrated by the appearance of the reuniting fleet, Hotham was forced to take flight. On the afternoon of the 14th the consorts made a prize of the British bomb ketch *Thunderer.*[160]

The morning of the 15th saw the French overhaul and take the *Senegal,* a sloop of war mounting sixteen guns. That same day the fleet anchored at latitude 39°, some twenty-five leagues off the coast of Cape May, where the *Languedoc* and *Marseilles* were set with jury-masts. While at anchor, the fleet was observed by Howe, who was on board the *Phoenix* (44 guns). Leaving the fifty-gun *Centurion* to gather and direct those of his dispersed vessels still at sea, Howe then headed for the fleet's rendezvous at Sandy Hook. He arrived there on August 17 and found most of the ships riding at anchor.[161]

On August 16, at 3:00 P.M., the *César* (74 guns), commanded by M. de Raimondis, encountered the *Isis* (50 guns), under Captain John Raynor, and gave chase. Neither ship had been injured to any extent by the storm, and in a short time the faster-sailing *César* was upon the smaller ship. For an hour and a half the two vessels engaged one another within pistol range. Aimed at the Britisher's rigging, Raimondis's fire inflicted severe damage to her sails, rigging, and masts, but killed only one man while wounding fourteen others. In contrast, Raynor employed the standard British tactic of sweeping the *César's* decks, and repeatedly hulled her. At length, with some sixty dead and one hundred wounded, among whom was Raimondis, who had lost his right arm, the *César* sheered off and ran before the wind. The *Isis,* incapable of pursuing due to the damage to her tops, limped back into Sandy Hook on August 17, where Raynor was commended by Howe and held up as an example for the admiral's officers. On August 22 the *César* put in at Boston, where the French proceeded to overrate the number of their opponent's guns.[162]

With the main French force depleted by the absence of the *César,* which was believed to be lost or bound for Boston as the king's instructions to the fleet commanded in case of accident or a threat from a superior opponent, d'Estaing and his captains were faced with the problem of what course to follow. The admiral's officers were certain, as was d'Estaing himself, that Howe and Byron would now combine forces, and chafing over Sullivan's failure to supply the fleet with anything near an adequate amount of water and victuals, they urged d'Estaing to set a course for Boston. To their disgust the admiral insisted upon honoring the promise he had given Sullivan by returning first to Rhode Island.[163] Howe's success had been far greater than he knew.

Notes

1. Washington to Sullivan, July 27, 1778, in Fitzpatrick, ed., *Writings of Washington,* XII, 237–38.

2. Washington to d'Estaing, July 26, 1778, in *Ibid.,* 232–33; Washington to Lafayette, July 27, 1778, in *Ibid.,* pp. 236–37.

3. Washington to Nathanael Greene, July 21, 1778, in *Ibid.,* pp. 199–200.

4. Greene, *Life of Greene,* II, 108.

5. Greene, *Life of Greene,* II, 108.

6. "Journal of Ebenezer Wild," *Proceedings of the Massachusetts Historical Society,* 2nd series, VI (1890–91), 113.

7. Washington to Lafayette, July 27, 1778, in Fitzpatrick, ed., *Writings of Washington,* XII, 237.

8. Lafayette to Washington, August 6, 1778, in Sparks, ed., *Letters to Washington,* II, 174.

9. John Laurens to Henry Laurens, August 4, 1778, in Laurens, *Army Correspondence,* p. 210.

10. John Laurens to Henry Laurens, August 4, 1778, in Laurens, *Army Correspondence,* p. 210.

11. *Ibid.,* Sullivan to General William Heath, July 29, 1778, in Hammond, ed., *Letters and Papers of Sullivan,* II, 143; Sullivan to d'Estaing, July 25, 1778, in *Ibid.,* III, 640–44.

12. John Laurens to Henry Laurens, August 4, 1778, in Laurens, *Army Correspondence,* pp. 210–12; d'Estaing to Sullivan, July 30, 1778, in Hammond, ed., *Letters and Papers of Sullivan,* II, 151; Mackenzie, *Diary,* II, 319–20.

13. Letter of d'Estaing quoted in Perkins, *France in the American Revolution,* p. 266.

14. Sullivan to d'Estaing, July 26, 1778, in Hammond, ed., *Letters and Papers of Sullivan,* III, 640.

15. Freeman, *Washington,* V, 66.

16. D'Estaing to Sullivan, July 30, 1778, in Hammond, ed., *Letters and Papers of Sullivan,* II, 152.

17. Lafayette to Washington, August 6, 1778, in Sparks, ed., *Letters to Washington,* II, 174–75; d'Estaing to Washington, August 3, 1778, in *Ibid.,* p. 172; d'Estaing to Sullivan, July 31, 1778, in Hammond, ed., *Letters and Papers of Sullivan,* II, 155; Sullivan to Meshech Weare, August 4, 1778, in *Ibid.,* p. 180.

18. D'Estaing to Sullivan, August 3, 1778, in *Ibid.,* p. 170; d'Estaing to Sullivan, August 4, 1778, in *Ibid.,* p. 174; d'Estaing to Washington, August 3, 1778, in Sparks. ed., *Letters to Washington,* II, 172; Freeman, *Washington,* V, 66.

19. Lafayette to Washington, August 6, 1778, in Sparks, ed., *Letters to Washington,* II, 175.

20. D'Estaing to Washington, August 3, 1778, in *Ibid.,* p. 172; d'Estaing to Sullivan, July 30, 1778, in Hammond, ed., *Letters and Papers of Sullivan,* II, 152.

21. Washington to Major General Horatio Gates, July 14, 1778, in Fitzpatrick, ed., *Writings of Washington,* XII, 177.

22. John Laurens to Henry Laurens, August 4, 1778, in Laurens, *Army Correspondence,* p. 215; Governor William Greene to Sullivan, August 14, 1778, in Hammond, ed., *Letters and Papers of Sullivan,* II, 209.

23. Washington to Sullivan, July 28, 1778, in *Ibid.,* p. 135; John Laurens to Washington, July 25, 1778, in Sparks, ed., *Letters to Washington,* II, 171; Asa Waterman to [?], July 23, 1778, Papers of Asa Waterman, Rhode Island Revolutionary War Deputy Commissioner, 1775–1781, Rhode Island State Ar-

chives; Peter Colt to Asa Waterman, July 28, 1778, Papers of Captain Asa Waterman, Rhode Island Revolutionary War Deputy Commissioner, 1775–1781, RIHS.

24. Sullivan to Washington, August 13, 1778, in Hammond, ed., *Letters and Papers of Sullivan,* II, 207.

25. State of Rhode Island and Providence Plantations, Council of War, July 29, 1778, printed broadside, Broadside File, RIHS.

26. Massachusetts Council to Sullivan, July 28, 1778, in Hammond, ed., *Letters and Papers of Sullivan,* II, 132–33.

27. Governor Jonathan Trumbull to Sullivan, July 25, 1778, in *Ibid,* p. 121.

28. Governor Trumbull to Sullivan, August 3, 1778, in *Ibid.,* pp. 171–72; Sullivan to Governor William Greene, August 18, 1778, in *Ibid.,* p. 229; *Connecticut Military Record: Records of Connecticut Men in the War of the Revolution,* compiled by authority of the General Assembly under direction of the Adjutants-General (Hartford, 1889), p. 430. Although Sullivan's letter to Governor Greene dated August 18 states that Connecticut had sent only 412 of her militiamen to his army, his statement may not have been quite true. Connecticut's muster rolls and pay rolls indicate that Colonel Chapman's regiment, composed of seven companies (a company being made up of approximately 100 men) joined the Rhode Island expedition (*Connecticut in the Revolution,* pp. 530–34), and this also seems to have been the case with the seven companies of Colonel Samuel McClellan's regiment. It should be noted that Sullivan's return of 412 men was probably made somewhere around the 18th, and by then large numbers of his volunteers had already deserted him.

29. Sullivan to Henry Laurens, August 6, 1778, in Hammond, ed., *Letters and Papers of Sullivan,* II, 181; Stiles, *Diary,* I, 294.

30. Meshech Weare to Sullivan, July 28, 1778, in Hammond, ed., *Letters and Papers of Sullivan,* II, 132.

31. Daniel Lyman to William Heath, August 11, 1778, in *Heath Papers, Massachusetts Historical Society Collections,* 7th series, Vol. IV, Part II (Boston: Massachusetts Historical Society, 1904), p. 246.

32. Washington to Sullivan, July 31, 1778, in Hammond, ed., *Letters and Papers of Sullivan,* II, 160.

33. Sullivan to d'Estaing, July 26, 1778, in *Ibid.,* III, 640; John Laurens to Henry Laurens, *Army Correspondence,* pp. 215–16.

34. Heath to Sullivan, September 6, 1778, in Hammond, ed., *Letters and Papers of Sullivan,* II, 308. Heath was in command of the Eastern Department and largely responsible for quartermaster duties.

35. Sullivan to Henry Laurens, August 1, 1778, in Hammond, ed., *Letters and Papers of Sullivan,* II, 166; Henry T. Tuckerman, *The Life of Silas Talbot, A Commodore in the Navy of the United States* (New York: J. C. Riker, 1850), p. 47.

36. Sullivan to Silas Talbot, July 27, 1778, *Rhode Island Historical Society Collections,* XXV (1932), 115.

37. *The Life and Surprising Adventures of Captain Silas Talbot* (London: printed by Barnard and Sultzer for Tegg and Castleman, 1803), pp. 34–35.

38. Sullivan to Glover, August 1, 1778, in William P. Upham, "A Memoir of General John Glover of Marblehead," *Historical Collections of the Essex Institute,* V (June 1863), 107.

39. George A. Billias, "General Glover's Role in the Battle of Rhode Island," *Rhode Island History,* XIX (April 1959), 34–35; George A. Billias, *General John Glover and His Marblehead Mariners* (New York: Holt, Rinehart and Winston, 1960), pp. 164–65.

40. Heath to Sullivan, July 29, 1778, in Hammond, ed., *Letters and Papers,* II, 144.

41. Lynn Montross, *Rag, Tag and Bobtail* (New York: Harper & Brothers, 1952), p. 293.

42. Rudy, "Rhode Island in the Revolution," p. 39.

43. Edwin Martin Stone, *Our French Allies* (Providence: Providence Press Co., 1884), p. 65.

44. Asa Waterman to Peter Colt, August 11, 1778, Waterman Papers, RIHS.

45. Often termed "Windmill Hill."

46. Mackenzie, *Diary,* I, 179–80; "Sketch of the North End of Rhode Island, with the disposition of the Advanced posts, Sentries, & patroles. 11th July 1778," in *Ibid.,* between pp. 308 and 309; George W. Cullum, *Historical Sketch of the Fortification Defenses of Narragansett Bay* (Washington, D.C., 1884), p. 11; Edward Field, *Revolutionary Defenses in Rhode Island* (Providence: Preston & Rounds, 1896), pp. 130, 138–39; "Map of Rhode Island and the various operations of the French fleet and American troops commanded by Major General Sullivan . . . ," in Preston, *Battle of Rhode Island,* p. 56; *Map of Military Operations on Rhode Island, 1778,* R.I. State Archives; *A Plan of Rhode Island with its Harbour & adjacent Parts shewing the situation of the British Ships & Forces when the French Fleet anchored off the Harbour July 29th, 1778,* British Museum. For a copy of the map from the British Museum, I am indebted to the kindness of Mr. Erwin Strasmick, Vice President of the Ross Mathews Corp. of Fall River, Mass.

47. The smallest of them was Green End, or Card's Redoubt, which mounted three large guns, and is still in an excellent state of preservation. Mackenzie, *Diary,* I, 292.

48. Bailey's Brook.

49. During the early seventeenth century the hill had been used as a fort and stronghold by the Narragansett sachem Miantonomi. The name of the hill had not, however, been derived from that figure, but from Wonumetonomy, the last sachem of the Aquidnicks. Stone, *Allies,* p. 113, n.

50. Mackenzie, *Diary,* I, 267, 291–92; Sullivan to the New Hampshire Committee of Safety, August 26, 1778, in Hammond, ed., *Letters and Papers,* II, 267–68; Sullivan to Henry Laurens, August 16, 1778, in *Ibid.,* p. 219; Sullivan to the President of Congress, August 31, 1778, in *Ibid.,* p. 281; [Fleet Greene], "Diary," *Historical Magazine,* IV, 36; Cullum, *Fortification Defenses,* p. 11; Field, *Revolutionary Defenses,* 130–34; "Map of Rhode Island . . . ," in Preston, *Battle of Rhode Island,* p. 56; *Map of Military Operations,* R.I. State Archives; *A Plan of Rhode Island . . . ,* British Museum.

51. Now the site of Fort Greene Park in Newport.

52. Both Cullum (*Fortification Defenses,* p. 13) and Field (*Revolutionary Defenses,* pp. 134–35), who culled not a little of his material from the former, erroneously assert that the British constructed this line during the siege in response to the fire of the American batteries on Honeyman's Hill. In doing

so, they confuse it with Pigot's strengthening of his position by means of raising batteries near Brenton's Neck and the construction of a line of abatis in
front of the outer works, in addition to a rebuilding and improvement of a
large portion of the outer line itself. Mackenzie, *Diary,* II, 332, 351–52. Mackenzie definitely states that this line was planned as early as September of
1777 (I, 180).

53. Mackenzie, *Diary,* I, 179–80; Sullivan to the President of Congress, August 31, 1778, in Hammond, ed., *Letters and Papers,* II, 281; Cullum,
Fortification Defenses, p. 13; "Map of Rhode Island . . . ," in Preston, *Battle
of Rhode Island,* p. 56; *Map of Military Operations,* R. I. State Archives; *A
Plan of Rhode Island . . . ,* British Museum.

54. When occupied by the Americans, they had termed it Fort Liberty.

55. The odd name originates in the fact that the large boulders which cover
the area are said to resemble dumplings from a distance. Federal Writers'
Project, *Rhode Island: A Guide,* p. 432.

56. Mackenzie, *Diary,* I, 308, II, 318; "Part of Conanicut Island,"in *Ibid.,* I,
between pp. 222 and 223; Taylor, *Campaign on Rhode Island,* sheet e; Cullum, *Fortification Defenses,* p. 12; Field, *Revolutionary Defenses,* pp. 83,
131–34; *A Plan of Rhode Island . . . ,* British Museum; Rider, "Review of
Field's *Revolutionary Defenses,"* XVI (1896), 73. Cullum, in his "Map of Narragansett Bay, R.I., 1778," which appears in *Fortification Defenses,* incor-
rectly shows another redoubt on Conanicut, near Beaver Tail, and Field (p.
117) also maintains that such a redoubt existed. For a refutation of this, see
Rider ("Review," pp. 74–75) and consult contemporary charts. In addition,
Cullum (p. 12) erroneously states that the British also guarded the West Passage by occupying a battery built by the Americans on a promontory at Bon-
net Point on the Narragansett shore. This position, he asserts (as does a
plaque on the grounds of the well-preserved site), was abandoned by the British upon the movement of d'Estaing's fleet into the bay due to the fear that
its garrison would be cut off. No contemporary accounts or documents which
this writer has been able to locate substantiate any of this. In addition, isolated on the mainland as it was, it seems unlikely that such a gun position
would have gone unmolested by the patriot forces. Should a retreat from the
battery have become necessary, it would have been impossible for the garrison to descend with any speed from the almost sheer drop of the promontory
to the beach, in order to escape from the mainland to the shelter of the
British-held islands. Militarily the situation would have been disastrous.
While the battery appears to date from the Revolutionary period, the story of
a British occupation must be dismissed as apocryphal.

57. Mackenzie, *Diary,* I, 180; "Map of Rhode Island . . . ," in Preston,
Battle of Rhode Island, p. 56; *Map of Military Operations . . . ,* R.I. State
Archives; *A Plan of Rhode Island . . . ,'* British Museum.

58. *A Plan of Rhode Island . . . ,* British Museum.

59. Rudy, "Rhode Island in the Revolution," p. 81.

60. *A Plan of Rhode Island . . . ,* British Museum; *Polk's Atlas,*
pp. 40–41. These observations rest primarily upon personal inspection of the
terrain.

61. Sullivan to d'Estaing, July 26, 1778, in Hammond, *Letters and Papers,*
III, 640–44.

62. Sullivan to d'Estaing, July 26, 1778, in Hammond, ed., *Letters and Papers,* III, 644.

63. D'Estaing to Sullivan, July 30, 1778, in Hammond, ed., *Letters and Papers,* II, 151–52; *Extrait de journal d'un officier marine avec le Comte d'Estaing dans les Etats Unis* (n.p., n.d.), 9–10; John Laurens to Henry Laurens, August 4, 1778, in Laurens, *Army Correspondence,* pp. 213–14.

64. No known document reveals what these changes might have been, nor can they be deduced from the events that subsequently occurred.

65. John Laurens to Henry Laurens, August 4, 1778, in Laurens, *Army Correspondence,* p. 214.

66. Whittemore, *A General of the Revolution,* p. 91.

67. Mary Almy, "Mrs. Almy's Journal," *Newport Historical Magazine,* I (July 1880), 18–19; [Greene], "Diary," *Historical Magazine,* IV, 71–72.

68. In October of 1777 Pigot had authorized the formation of a Loyalist association to aid in the defense of Rhode Island. At that time some 180 men were formed into three volunteer companies under the command of Colonel Joseph Wanton, Jr. Mackenzie, *Diary,* I, 201.

69. Mackenzie, *Diary,* II, 326.

70. Edward J. Lowell, *The Hessians and the Other German Auxiliaries of Great Britain in the Revolutionary War* (New York, 1884), pp. 218–19.

71. [?] to [?], September 8, 1778, in William L. Stone, ed., *Letters of German Soldiers in the American Revolution* (Albany: Joel Munsell's Sons, 1891), p. 228.

72. Mackenzie, *Diary,* II, 372; Popp, *Diary of Stephan Popp,* p. 12; John Laurens to Henry Laurens, August 4, 1778, in Laurens, *Army Correspondence,* p. 216; *Providence Gazette,* August 1, 1778.

73. Pigot to Clinton, August 31, 1778, in "Centennial Celebration of the Battle of Rhode Island . . . ," *Rhode Island Historical Tracts,* No. 6 (Providence: Sidney S. Rider, 1878), p. 83; Stedman, *American War,* II, 29; Mackenzie, *Diary,* II, 334.

74. Willcox, "British Strategy," *Journal of Modern History,* XIX, 115.

75. Mackenzie, *Diary,* II, 332–33.

76. *Ibid.,* pp. 322–23.

77. Mackenzie, *Diary,* II, 319–21; Popp, *Diary of Stephan Popp,* p. 11; [Greene], "Diary," *Historical Magazine,* IV, 72; Max von Eelking, "Military Operations in Rhode Island: The Siege of Newport," in "Centennial Celebration of the Battle of Rhode Island," *Rhode Island Historical Tracts,* No. 6, pp. 40–41; Pigot to Clinton, August 31, 1778, in *Ibid.,* 84.

78. Mackenzie, *Diary,* II, 326, 329; von Eelking, "Military Operations," *Rhode Island Historical Tracts,* No. 6, p. 43.

79. [Greene], "Diary," *Historical Magazine,* IV, 72.

80. Mackenzie, *Diary,* II, 328.

81. *Ibid.,* pp. 325, 328–29; [Greene], "Diary," *Historical Magazine,* IV, 72, 104; Pigot to Clinton, August 31, 1778, in *Rhode Island Historical Tracts,* No. 6, p. 85.

82. Mackenzie, *Diary,* II, 328–29; Pigot to Clinton, August 31, 1778, in *Rhode Island Historical Tracts,* No. 6, p. 85; William Parker Cutler and Julia Perkins, *Life, Journals and Correspondence of Reverend Manasseh Cutler,* 2 vols. (Cincinnati: Robert Clarke & Co., 1888), I, 66.

83. Mackenzie, *Diary,* II, 329.

84. Almy, "Journal," *Newport Historical Magazine,* I, 19; [Greene], "Diary," *Historical Magazine,* IV, 72.

85. Mackenzie, *Diary,* II, 326, 332.

86. [Greene], "Diary," *Historical Magazine,* IV, 72; "Diary of Ezekiel Price," *New England Historical and Genealogical Register,* XIX (October, 1865), 334; Cutler and Perkins, *Manasseh Cutler,* II, 66.

87. [Greene], "Diary," *Historical Magazine,* IV, 72, 105; Mackenzie, *Diary,* II, 331–32; Popp, *Diary of Stephan Popp,* p. 11; Taylor, *Campaign on Rhode Island,* sheet e; d'Estaing to Sullivan, August 4, 1778, in Hammond, ed., *Letters and Papers,* II, 174.

88. Mackenzie, *Diary,* II, 319.

89. D'Estaing to Sullivan, July 31, 1778, in Hammond, ed., *Letters and Papers,* II, 154–55; General Ezekiel Cornell to Sullivan, July 31, 1778, in *Ibid.,* pp. 157–58; Sullivan to Jeremiah Powell, August 1, 1778, in *Ibid.,* pp. 163–64; Mackenzie, *Diary,* II, 321; [Greene], "Diary," *Historical Magazine,* IV, 72; *Extrait de journal,* p. 9; John Laurens to Henry Laurens, August 4, 1778, in Laurens, *Army Correspondence,* p. 212; *A Plan of Rhode Island,* British Museum.

90. Sullivan to Henry Laurens, August 1, 1778, in Hammond, ed., *Letters and Papers,* II, 166–67.

91. Mackenzie, *Diary,* II, 327–30; [Greene], "Diary," *Historical Magazine,* IV, 105; Almy, "Journal," *Newport Historical Magazine,* I, 20; d'Estaing to Sullivan, August 7, 1778, in Hammond, ed., *Letters and Papers,* II, 183–84; *A Plan of Rhode Island,* British Museum; Pigot to Clinton, August 31, 1778, in *Rhode Island Historical Tracts,* No. 6, p. 84; *Extrait de Journal,* pp. 10–11.

92. Mackenzie, *Diary,* II, 323–24, 330–31; von Eelking, "Military Operations," *Rhode Island Historical Tracts,* No. 6, p. 43.

93. Mackenzie, *Diary,* II, 331.

94. Almy, "Journal," *Newport Historical Magazine,* I, 22.

95. Mackenzie, *Diary,* II, 331, 333; [Greene], "Diary," *Historical Magazine,* IV, 105; *A Plan of Rhode Island,* British Museum.

96. Mackenzie, *Diary,* II, 326–27; [Greene], "Diary," *Historical Magazine,* IV, 72; Almy, "Journal," *Newport Historical Magazine,* I, 20–21.

97. Mackenzie, *Diary,* II, 322; Laurens to Henry Laurens, August 4, 1778, in Laurens, *Army Correspondence,* p. 215. Although Laurens wrote that the reconnaissance took place on July 31, his letter was not written until August 4 and is thus subject to some error in the recollection of a specific date. Mackenzie presumably recorded the events mentioned in his diary on the day of their occurrence; Mackenzie's date is followed in the text.

98. D'Estaing to Sullivan, August 3, 1778, in Hammond, ed., *Letters and Papers,* II, 171; Sullivan to d'Estaing, July 26, 1778, in *Ibid.,* pp. 642–44; John Laurens to Henry Laurens, August 22, 1778, in Laurens, *Army Correspondence,* p. 217.

99. Greene to Washington, August 28, 1778, in Greene, *Life of Greene,* II, 127.

100. Lafayette to d'Estaing, July 22, 1778, in Henri Doniol, *Histoire de la Participation de la France à l'establishment des Etats-Unis d'Amérique,* 6

vols. (Paris, 1884–92), VI, 402; Lafayette to d'Estaing, July 24, 1778, in *Ibid.*, pp. 409–10.

101. Gottschalk, *Lafayette*, II, 242.

102. "Journal of Ebenezer Wild," *Proceedings of the Massachusetts Historical Society*, 2nd series, VI, 113; Gottschalk, *Lafayette*, II, 244.

103. John Laurens to Henry Laurens, August 22, 1778, in Laurens, *Army Correspondence*, pp. 217–18; Gottschalk, *Lafayette*, II, 244–45; Comte de Cambis, *"Extraits du journal tenu par le Comte de Cambis à bord du Languedoc,"* in Doniol, *Histoire*, III, 375.

104. Apparently the potential threat from Howe and Byron weighed heavily upon him throughout this period as well as later.

105. D'Estaing to Sullivan, August 4, 1778, in Hammond, ed., *Letters and Papers*, II, 173.

106. Gottschalk, *Lafayette*, II, 246.

107. John Laurens to Henry Laurens, August 22, 1778, in Laurens, *Army Correspondence*, p. 218.

108. Lafayette to d'Estaing, August 5, 1778, in Doniol, *Histoire*, VI, 414; John Laurens to Henry Laurens, August 22, 1778, in Laurens, *Army Correspondence*, p. 218.

109. John Laurens to Henry Laurens, August 22, 1778, in Laurens, *Army Correspondence*, p. 218.

110. Lafayette to d'Estaing, August 5, 1778, in Doniol, *Histoire*, VI, 415.

111. *Ibid.*, pp. 415–16.

112. *Ibid.*

113. Gottschalk, *Lafayette*, II, 247.

114. *Ibid.*

115. Lafayette to Washington, August 6, 1778, in Sparks, ed., *Letters to Washington*, II, 175.

116. D'Estaing to Sullivan, August 7, 1778, in Hammond, ed., *Letters and Papers*, II, 184.

117. *Ibid.*

118. Nathaniel Wright Stephenson and Waldo Hilary Dunn, *George Washington*, 2 vols. (New York: Oxford University Press, 1940), II, 107.

119. Washington to Sullivan, July 27, 1778, in Fitzpatrick, ed., *Writings of Washington*, XII, 238.

120. *Ibid.*

121. John Laurens to Henry Laurens, August 22, 1778, in Laurens, *Army Correspondence*, p. 219.

122. Lafayette to d'Estaing, August 8, 1778, in Doniol, *Histoire*, VI, 416–17.

123. John Laurens to Henry Laurens, August 22, 1778, in Laurens, *Army Correspondence*, p. 219; d'Estaing to Sullivan, August 7, 1778, in Hammond, ed., *Letters and Papers*, II, 183.

124. Mackenzie, *Diary*, II, 338–39, 379; [Greene], "Diary," *Historical Magazine*, IV, 105; Pigot to Clinton, August 31, 1778, in *Rhode Island Historical Tracts*, No. 6, p. 85; *Extrait de journal*, pp. 11–12; von Eelking, "Military Operations," in *Rhode Island Historical Tracts*, No. 6, p. 45; d'Estaing to Sullivan, August 7, 1778, in Hammond, ed., *Letters and Papers*, II, 184; Popp, *Diary of Stephan Popp*, p. 13; John Laurens to Henry Laurens, August 22,

1778, in Laurens, *Army Correspondence,* p. 219; *A Plan of Rhode Island,* British Museum.

125. Mackenzie, *Diary,* II, 340–41; [Greene], "Diary," *Historical Magazine,* IV, 105; Almy, "Journal," *Newport Historical Magazine,* I, 25–26; *A Plan of Rhode Island,* British Museum.

126. Mackenzie, *Diary,* II, 339–40, 346; Pigot to Clinton, August 31, 1778, in *Rhode Island Historical Tracts,* No. 6, p. 85.

127. Lafayette to Washington, August 25, 1778, in Sparks, ed., *Letters to Washington,* II, 182; Sullivan to Henry Laurens, August 10, 1778, in Hammond, ed., *Letters and Papers,* II, 191.

128. Cutler and Perkins, *Manasseh Cutler,* II, 65–66.

129. Sullivan to Heath, August 11, 1778, in Hammond, ed., *Letters and Papers,* II, 197.

130. Sullivan to Henry Laurens, August 10, 1778, in *Ibid.,* p. 191; Sullivan to Heath, August 11, 1778, in *Ibid.,* pp. 198–99; John Laurens to Henry Laurens, August 22, 1778, in Laurens, *Army Correspondence,* p. 220.

131. "Journal of Ebenezer Wild," *Proceedings of the Massachusetts Historical Society,* 2nd series, VI, 114; Noah Robinson, Journal of a Six Months' Campaign, RIHS.

132. Noah Robinson, Journal, RIHS. Robinson was a member of the company under command of Captain Caleb Richardson.

133. Lafayette to Washington, August 25, 1778, in Sparks, ed., *Letters to Washington,* II, 182; d'Estaing to Congress, August 26, 1778, in Jared Sparks, ed., *The Writings of Washington,* 12 vols. (Boston: Russell, Odiorne, & Metcalf, and Hilliard, Gray & Co., 1834), VI, 31 n.

134. John Laurens to Henry Laurens, August 22, 1778, in Laurens, *Army Correspondence,* p. 220.

135. D'Estaing to Congress, August 26, 1778, in Sparks, ed., *The Writings of Washington,* VI, 31 n.; d'Estaing to Sullivan, August 21, 1778, in Hammond, ed., *Letters and Papers,* II, 241.

136. *Extrait de journal,* p. 13.

137. D'Estaing to Congress, August 26, 1778, in Sparks, ed., *The Writings of Washington,* VI, 30 n; Mackenzie, *Diary,* II, 341.

138. [Greene], "Diary," *Historical Magazine,* IV, 105; Popp, *Diary of Stephan Popp,* p. 12.

139. Mackenzie, *Diary,* II, 342.

140. Almy, "Journal," *Newport Historical Magazine,* I, 27.

141. D'Estaing to Congress, August 26, 1778, in Sparks, ed., *The Writings of Washington,* VI, 30 n.; *Extrait de journal,* pp. 13–14; Mackenzie, *Diary,* II, 343.

142. O'Beirne, *The Fleet under Lord Howe,* p. 27; Mackenzie, *Diary,* II, 342.

143. Mackenzie, *Diary,* II, 342; O'Beirne, *The Fleet under Lord Howe,* p. 27; Almy, "Journal," *Newport Historical Magazine,* I, 27.

144. Clinton, *American Rebellion,* pp. 101–02; Mackenzie, *Diary,* II, 332, 344; Willcox, "British Strategy in America, 1778," *Journal of Modern History,* XIX, 114; Willcox, *Potrait of a General,* p. 244, 5 n.; Gruber, "Richard Lord Howe," in Billias, ed., *Washington's Opponents,* pp. 249–50; Major John

Bowater to the Earl of Denbigh, July 31, 1778, in Marion Balderstom and David Syrett, eds., *The Lost War: Letters from British Officers during the American Revolution* (New York: Horizon Press, 1975), p. 167.

145. Ira D. Gruber, *The Howe Brothers and the American Revolution* (Chapel Hill: University of North Carolina Press, 1972), pp. 311–12; Gruber, "Richard Lord Howe," in Billias, ed., *Washington's Opponents,* p. 250; MSS attached to a letter from L. Porter to [?], September 14, 1778, [Declaration of Captain Venture, August 1, 1778], Peck MSS, RIHS; Intelligence from the American Office, September 13, 1778, in John W. Fortescue, ed., *The Correspondence of King George III,* 6 vols. (London, 1927–28), IV, 194.

146. O'Beirne, *The Fleet under Lord Howe,* p. 29.

147. They were the 23rd Regiment, Royal Welsh Fusiliers, who had volunteered to serve as marines. Mackenzie, *Diary,* II, 344.

148. D'Estaing to Congress, August 26, 1778, in Sparks, ed., *The Writings of Washington,* VI, 30 n.; *Extrait de journal,* pp. 13–15; Whittemore, *A General of the Revolution,* p. 96.

149. D'Estaing to Sullivan, August 21, 1778, in Hammond, ed., *Letters and Papers,* II, 241; Lyman to Heath, August 10, 1778, in *Heath Papers,* Part II, 245.

150. D'Estaing to Congress, August 26, 1778, in Sparks, ed., *The Writings of Washington,* VI, 30 n.; Lafayette to d'Estaing, August 10, 1778, in Doniol, *Histoire,* VI, 418; Lafayette to Washington, August 25, 1778, in Sparks. ed., *Letters to Washington,* II, 182. Although Sullivan's letter does not appear in Hammond, its essence can be determined from the above documents.

151. D'Estaing to Sullivan, August 21, 1778, in Hammond, ed., *Letters and Papers,* II, 240–41.

152. D'Estaing to Congress, August 26, 1778, in Sparks, ed., *The Writings of Washington,* VI, 30 n.

153. Washington to d'Estaing, August 8, 1778, in Fitzpatrick, ed., *Writings of Washington,* XII, 291–93. Fitzpatrick accompanies the letter with a note stating that it arrived at Rhode Island after Howe's ships had already appeared.

154. Count de Cambis to Sullivan, August 20, 1778, in Hammond, ed., *Letters and Papers,* II, 238; Mackenzie, *Diary,* II, 344; *Extrait de journal,* pp. 15–16.

155. *Extrait de journal,* pp. 15–16; [Greene], "Diary," *Historical Magazine,* IV, 105; Almy, "Journal," *Newport Historical Magazine,* I, 27–28; O'Beirne, *The Fleet under Lord Howe,* pp. 29–30; Mackenzie, *Diary,* II, 344, 346, 353; Pigot to Clinton, August 31, 1778, in *Rhode Island Historical Tracts,* No. 6, p. 86.

156. *Extrait de journal,* p. 16; O'Beirne, *The Fleet under Lord Howe,* p. 20; Mackenzie, *Diary,* II, 344.

157. Mackenzie, *Diary,* II, 345.

158. O'Beirne, *The Fleet under Lord Howe,* pp. 30–31; Gruber, "Richard Lord Howe," in Billias, ed., *Washington's Opponents,* p. 250; *Extrait de journal,* pp. 16–20; Mackenzie, *Diary,* II, 345.

159. O'Beirne, *The Fleet under Lord Howe,* pp. 32–34; Gruber, *The Howe Brothers,* pp. 315–16; Gruber, "Richard Lord Howe," in Billias, ed.,

Washington's Opponents, pp. 250–51; *Extrait de journal,* pp. 20–21; *New York Journal,* September 7, 1778, in Moore, *Diary of the American Revolution,* II, 85–86.

160. *Extrait de journal,* pp. 22–23; O'Beirne, *The Fleet under Lord Howe,* pp. 34–35; William Stewart to William Goddard, September 10, 1778, Military Papers, V, 35, RIHS; *N.Y. Journal,* in Moore, *Diary of the Revolution,* II, 86.

161. *Extrait de journal,* p. 23; O'Beirne, *The Fleet under Lord Howe,* p. 34; *N.Y. Journal,* in Moore, *Diary of the Revolution,* II, 86; Stedman, *The American War,* II, 30.

162. O'Beirne, *The Fleet under Lord Howe,* pp. 35–36; Stedman, *The American War,* II, 31; Heath, *Memoirs,* p. 202; Carl Leopold Baurmeister, *Revolution in America: Confidential Letters and Journals 1776–1784 of Adjutant General Major Baurmeister of the Hessian Forces,* trans. and annotated by Bernhard A. Uhlendorf (New Brunswick, New Jersey: Rutgers University Press, 1957), p. 201; Charles A. Moré, *The Chevalier de Pontgibaud, a French Volunteer,* trans. and ed. by Robert B. Douglas (Paris: Charles Carrington, 1898), pp. 67–68; Anne Rowe Cunningham, ed., *Letters and Diary of John Rowe, Boston Merchant, 1759–1762, 1764–1779* (Boston: W. B. Clarke, Co., 1903), p. 320.

163. *Extrait de journal,* p. 24; Lafayette to Washington, August 25, 1778, in Sparks, ed., *Letters to Washington,* II, 183–84; d'Estaing to Sullivan, August 21, 1778, in Hammond, ed., *Letters and Papers,* II, 241–42.

VII

"To Combat All These Misfortunes . . ."

WHILE D'ESTAING AND HOWE struggled for control of the sea and Sullivan fretted over the fleet's absence, fearful that the resulting delay might permit the British to relieve Newport and put an end to the expedition, the American troops remained on Rhode Island and continued to grow in number.[1] On August 8, after a period of much indecision which he credited to the state of his health, John Hancock, ever seeking to display his martial skills, left Boston with his suite to take command of his state's militia.[2] Two days later, probably much to his pleasure, the army's countersign became "Hancock."[3] By August 11 Sullivan's army numbered 10,122 men, exclusive of some five to six hundred New Hampshire volunteers and some other corps.[4] Among the recruits were Sullivan's brothers, Eben (who served as an aide to the general) and James.[5] Also serving as an aide to Sullivan was Major Daniel Lyman, who had been recommended to Sullivan by Heath in the hope that Lyman would keep an eye on the proceedings and accurately inform him of their development.[6] Lyman was soon won over by his new chief. Even James Otis, tragically robbed of a brilliant mind by the combined effects of chronic alcoholism and a blow to the head during a 1769 tavern brawl with a group of Tories, came to wander about the camp.[7]

As to the effectiveness of the large body of militia that had rallied to him, Sullivan was not deceived.[8] Of this horde Lafayette's aide, the Chevalier de Pontgibaud, drew a pointed and perhaps somewhat overstated picture when he wrote:

> I have never seen a more laughable spectacle; all the tailors and apothecaries in the country must have been called out, I should think;—one could recognize them by their round wigs. They were mounted on bad nags, and looked like a flock of ducks in cross-belts. The infantry was no better than the cavalry, and appeared to be cut after the same pattern. I guessed that these warriors were more anxious to eat up our supplies than to make a close acquaintance with the enemy. . . .[9]

Sullivan's anxiety to get on with the work ahead of him before events could take another turn for the worse, plus his belief that his army was strong enough to begin operations without the French, led him on the evening of August 11 to issue marching orders for six o'clock the following morning. That same night the storm that had struck the fleets hit the island and raged all through the 12th and 13th. Its violence forced Sullivan to postpone his advance. Most of his camp's tents were leveled, and his stock of ammunition was almost totally destroyed. His men were forced to lie on the ground as the rain and wind beat down upon them. Many men and horses, unable to endure more, died of exposure.[10] Behind the lines around Newport, the British fared almost as badly, particularly in the case of the seamen.[11]

Sullivan's position was desperate. If the British atacked he would be forced to rely on the bayonet, as would the enemy, for firelocks did not function in wet weather. The American commander frankly doubted the ability of his militia to withstand a rush of cold steel, and with Seconnet passage churning, his line of retreat was cut off. To Washington he wrote, "to retreat is impossible; therefore we must conquer or perish." [12] Greene too believed that the army was then in peril should the British make a concentrated attack.[13] On the 12th Pigot considered precisely such a measure, but apparently expecting the return of Howe and the relief of the garrison, he rejected it.[14]

Ever mindful of his need for a success, Sullivan continually reminded his correspondents of the bad luck which had dogged the expedition.[15] To Governor Greene he wrote that should the expedition fail, "I wish you & your assembly to witness for my Character against a Censorious world who will take pleasure to Blast my Reputation for being unsuccessful Even though they know it to be unavoidable." [16]

When the weather cleared on the morning of August 14, Sullivan gave orders for his army to be ready to move forward the next day at 6:00 A.M.[17] On the morning of the 15th the army marched south at seven o'clock, with Varnum's brigade taking the West Road and Glover's the East, while between them moved the brigades assigned to Colonels Ezekiel Cornell and Christopher Greene. Commanding the right wing was Nathanael Greene, while Lafayette had the left. Behind Christopher Greene and Cornell marched the two brigades of the second line under Hancock. Still farther back were the two reserve regiments under General West. Flanking the army on the left was General Tyler with his Connecticut troops, while General Whipple with his New Hampshiremen covered the right. Behind them Tyler and Whipple each left a hundred men under one of their field officers to protect the flanks of the reserve.

With the units moved their artillery. Two heavy guns were mounted on field carriages for transportation down the West Road, while two more were placed on the East Road. Advanced at least a mile ahead of the main body was the light corps under Colonel Henry Beekman Livingston. Serving with him were Laurens and Major Talbot.[18] Leading the men was their overall commander. In the words of one of Sullivan's admiring officers, "immediately on marching the General Rode in front to reconnoitre on the west Road, and after that proceeded to go on the east—attended by two hundred horsemen to protect, and defend, a man who is an ornament to the character of a Soldier." [19] Thus arranged and vigilant, Sullivan's columns could quickly deploy to meet any attack.

By two o'clock the Americans reached the vicinity of Honeyman's Hill, about two miles from the British lines, facing the northern portion of the Green End sector. There the rebels pitched camp, stationed advanced posts, and began to throw up fieldworks for their protection. [20]

Sullivan's position, although it was the one selected by a council of war on July 25, represented a poor choice of ground from which to conduct a siege. [21] Between Honeyman's Hill and Bliss Hill, where the Green End line was built, lay Easton's Pond and its tributary which the British had dammed, turning much of the floor of the ravine into marshy ground. When parallels were dug on the face of Honeyman's Hill and extended downhill to approach Green End, the Americans would have to contend with plunging fire from the British artillery on the opposite heights. Thus, from their elevated position the enemy would be able to fire their shot along a trajectory that could place their missiles squarely inside the American trenches.

Even more serious was the fact that should it become necessary to storm the British lines, such an attack would mean charging down Honeyman's Hill, crossing the water-sogged ravine under enemy cannon fire, and then ascending to Green End in the face of both artillery and massed musketry. Even if such an assault were successful, the British could retire to their stronghold on Tomini Hill, which lay on still higher ground. [22]

If Sullivan had approached the British lines from the north, facing Tomini, rather than from the east, he would then have been in a more favorable position. There he could have taken Green End in the flank, although Tomini might have been able to hold out. Despite the fact that the odds against his success would still have been great, they would at least have been improved. On the north he would be on level ground,

COLONEL CHRISTOPHER GREENE

avoiding the problem of the ravine.[23] There the most logical plan of procedure would comprise the capture of the outworks in front of Tomini and then, in a precipitate rush, the scaling of the steep front of the hill itself to capture the redoubt on the summit. Such an attack would be costly, but perhaps less so than assaulting Green End and then taking Tomini. Once in possession of Tomini, the Americans would hold the ground and Pigot's troops would be in the open with no position at which to rally for a successful stand between Tomini and the town of Newport itself. Sullivan might well have had the victory for which he longed, yet his own decision helped to prevent him from realizing it.

On the night of August 16 Sullivan began his siege works on Honeyman's Hill with the construction of a battery for four guns. On that day Pigot had opened an ineffectual bombardment of Honeyman's Hill, which increased in its briskness on August 17 in response to the Americans' effort to raise their battery.[24] By the 17th the British had begun to find their enemy's range. As the Reverend Manasseh Cutler, who had volunteered to serve as chaplain to General Titcomb's brigade, noted in his diary:

> found our situation not very safe or agreeable. Stood by the Marquis [Lafayette] when a cannon ball just passed us. Was pleased with his firmness, but found I had nothing to boast of my own, and as I had no business in danger concluded to stay no longer lest I should happen to pay too dear for my curiosity.[25]

Pigot had begun to lose hope. He was no longer certain that he could successfully hold Sullivan back, and on August 16 he wrote to Clinton asking him whether he intended to come to the garrison's relief or send transports in which Pigot could evacuate his men. For the first time he also grimly mentioned the possibility of surrender.[26]

In contrast, the Americans were sanguine. Lieutenant Colonel Paul Revere, an artillery officer in the Massachusetts militia and a veteran of Spencer's expedition, wrote to his wife assuring her that the siege would soon be over and telling her that "I am in high health and spirits, & [so is] our Army. The Enemy dare not show their heads." [27] Yet all was not well. From the first, Sullivan was beset by desertions among his militia, and he was forced to beg for more men from the New England states.[28] From Connecticut came a promise of six companies and forty light-horsemen, while Massachusetts reluctantly pledged nine hundred men.[29] Resources were running low, and each state looked jealously to its own defense. Only after a considerable amount of cajolery did Rhode Island, which had the most to gain by a victory, agree to send the remaining half of its militia.[30] Though desertions continued, Sullivan expansively wrote to Governor Greene of Rhode Island that "the Resolve of your Council has put it Compleatly in my power to Reduce the Enemy without further assistance." [31] Whether Sullivan believed his own words was another question.

On the night of August 18 the Americans began raising a five-gun battery on the left of their first work and in a direct line with it. Work was also started on the trenches, or "parallels," by which Sullivan could gradually draw closer to the British line. All the while Pigot's guns thundered across the valley in an effort to obstruct the American construction work.[32] From the British lines Captain Mackenzie observed the efforts of the rebels and wrote, "It appears . . . that they intend to make their principal attack upon our right, by way of Green-end. They certainly can bring their Batteries nearer on that side; but the more they advance with their approaches, the more our ground commands them. We are strong there. . . ." [33]

While the Americans had prepared to march south and labored on their emplacements, Pigot's men kept at the work of strengthening the British line. Beginning on August 10 the troops started cutting down trees in the orchards near the works and placing them in front of the outer intrenchments to form an abatis from Green End to Tomini Hill. Three days later Pigot began construction of a line of breastworks some six feet thick and four and a half feet high. Started forty feet back from the abatis, the breastworks were to run from Green End to Tomini and thus protect the men near the redoubts that formed the outer line. On August 14 an abatis was also laid along Easton's Beach from the pond to the redoubt anchoring the inner line, thus further covering the gap on the right between the two lines of works. On the left of the outer line, the area entrusted to General von Lossberg, the German built a flèche in front of Little Tomini on August 16 and stationed two six-pounders there with a detachment of seamen to man them.[34]

The battery that had been constructed on the left of the American siege line was completed by the morning of August 19. At approximately 8:00 A.M., as the fog cleared away, Sullivan's four eighteen-pounders commenced a cannonade of the British lines, forcing Pigot to move his encampment on the outer line farther back from the fortifications and silencing a small battery. The British too had worked their guns to effect, striking the American battery a number of times, wounding two men and killing another.[35]

As the American approaches crept forward on August 20, d'Estaing's crippled fleet returned to Rhode Island's waters. At 2:00 P.M. the ships became visible to the Americans, and shortly after five o'clock they once again dropped anchor off Brenton's Point. While American spirits initially soared, those in the British camp, despite the brave pretenses of such men as Captain Mackenzie, drooped even lower.[36]

Anxiously Sullivan awaited the chance to implement a plan for reembarking a large part of his army and landing it on the southern part of the island at Brenton's Neck behind the enemy lines. The fleet, the mainspring of the operation, could cover the assault.[37] But it was not to be. As the Reverend Cutler put it, "our most sanguine hopes were cropped in the bud." [38]

Through the Count de Cambis, d'Estaing informed Sullivan

that due to the damage his ships had sustained, he intended to approach no nearer to Rhode Island and that he would sail to Boston for repairs, taking the three frigates and the brigantine in the East Channel with him. Immediately Sullivan protested the admiral's decision and implored him to remain for twenty-four hours in order to complete the conquest of the island.[39] D'Estaing was not as certain of such an easy success, however. As he later wrote to Washington, "it was . . . difficult to persuade oneself that about six thousand men well entrenched and with a fort before which they had dug trenches could be taken either in twenty-four hours or in two days." [40]

On the evening of the 20th Nathanael Greene and Lafayette boarded the *Languedoc* as Sullivan's emissaries in a futile effort to persuade d'Estaing to stay. In response to their representations d'Estaing agreed to call a council of his captains, at which their call for the fleet to sail to Boston, as their government's instructions required, was unanimously reaffirmed. Their reasons were not without merit, for Byron was now definitely known to be off the coast, and the *Languedoc* and *Marseilles* were in no condition for a fight. In addition, even some of the American pilots serving with the French advised them to sail for Boston. The most that the council proposed to do at Rhode Island was aid in the evacuation of the American army to the mainland.[41]

Added to the logic of the captains' arguments, there may also have been another reason for d'Estaing's surrender to the council's decision. As John Laurens saw it, "the Count's hands were tied. The cabal of marine officers, who wish his destruction because he was introduced from the land service into their corps, left him, it is said, no choice." [42] In this judgment Greene concurred, and in hope of giving d'Estaing the courage to defy his captains' resolve, as well as a justification for doing so, the American general drew up a protest during the early hours of August 21 while still on board the *Languedoc*.[43] A capable diplomat as well as a soldier, Greene delivered to d'Estaing a paper which Henry Laurens, president of Congress, subsequently termed "a sensible and spirited Remonstrance." [44] As such, its tone was far different from one that was soon to follow it.

Professing to believe that d'Estaing himself wished to remain and continue the siege but had been forced to give up the attempt by the naval officers who desired to discredit him, Sullivan wrote the admiral a harsh letter on behalf of his officers.[45] Before it could be delivered, d'Estaing's ships weighed anchor shortly after midnight on August 22 and set sail for Boston.[46]

On the day of d'Estaing's departure Sullivan called a council of his officers, during which a formal protest of the French action was drawn up and signed by the American generals, including Greene and Hancock.[47] Tactlessly framed, the document asserted that the Americans had undertaken the Rhode Island campaign only because of promised aid from the French, and that Sullivan's army had been needlessly abandoned and left exposed to a disaster. With national sensitivities already unduly aroused, the door to further ill will was opened even more when the Americans claimed that

> the honor of the French nation must be injured by their fleet abandoning their allies upon an island, in the midst of an expedition agreed to by the Count himself. This must make such an unfavorable impression on the minds of Americans at large, and create such jealousies between them and their hitherto esteemed allies, as will in a great measure frustrate the good intentions of His Most Christian Majesty and the American Congress, who have mutually endeavored to promote the greatest harmony and confidence between the French people and the Americans.[48]

In concluding, Sullivan and his officers termed the action of the French fleet

> derogatory to the honor of France, contrary to the intentions of His Most Christian Majesty and the interest of his nation, and destructive in the highest degree to the welfare of the United States of America, and highly injurious to the alliance formed between the two nations.[49]

Although his fellow officers explained that they did not expect him to add his signature to the protest, and that he had been called to attend the council only because they did not wish to act without his knowledge, Lafayette was incensed. Exactly what form his reaction took is uncertain, but reputedly he clapped his hand on the hilt of his sword and proclaimed that his native land was dearer to him than America could ever be.[50] That day he wrote to d'Estaing in a melodramatic vein, "every word which will hereafter be pronounced I will expect to be the very one I will feel called upon to avenge." [51]

When the council ended, Laurens put to sea in a privateer to overtake the French fleet and deliver the American communications. Failing to catch up with d'Estaing, Laurens returned on the 23rd. The protest, along with Sullivan's letter, was forwarded to General Heath in Boston with a request that he deliver the documents when the French arrived.[52]

On August 23 the Americans opened two more batteries, and these, in addition to the two which had already seen service, engaged the British defenders in a day-long bombardment.[53] Yet Sullivan now had only 8,174 men, some 5,000 of whom were militia, with which to capture Pigot's heavily intrenched position.[54] With the departure of the French fleet, Sullivan's army dwindled rapidly. As Nathanael Greene wrote to Washington, "it struck such a panic among the militia and volunteers that they began to desert in shoals. The fleet no sooner set sail than they began to be alarmed for their safety. This misfortune damped the hopes of our army. . . ." [55] By August 24 Sullivan was moved to state in his general orders that "it is with grate Grief & astonishment, the Genl finds that grate numbers of Volinteers are about to quit the Island at this Time & to give america a Lasting Proof of their Want of firmness and Bravery." [56] That same day Major Samuel Ward, Jr., of the 1st Rhode Island Regiment, Christopher Greene's command, wrote bitterly to his wife:

two Companies of Volunteers from Massachusetts went off yestertay in Genl. all the Volunteers are gone and are going—

> campaigning does not suit such people and then tis really
> difficult for them to be so long from their Bussiness, an atten-
> tion to which is necessary you know in every Man—am I not
> very generous to apologise so candidly for Men who perhaps are
> leaving Me in the *lurch* I know you wont so readily excuse
> them—" [57]

One of those who left the army was John Hancock, who
asserted that his efforts in Boston might be of service to
d'Estaing. Promising to return, the former president of Congress made it known that his visit to his home town and the
fleet could help to hasten the fleet's repairs and its possible
reappearance in Rhode Island's waters.[58] At Hancock's request, Lafayette furnished him with a letter of introduction to
the admiral in which Lafayette referred to the Bostonian as a
"living Brutus." [59] But privately Lafayette wrote d'Estaing
that Hancock's decision might well be motivated by his "little
eagerness for English bullets." [60]

In general orders issued on August 24, Sullivan once again
gave vent to his resentment of d'Estaing's departure and attempted to rally the spirits of his men by proclaiming:

> The General cannot help lamenting the sudden & unexpected
> departure of the French Fleet as he finds it has a tendency to
> discourage some who place great dependence upon the assist-
> ance of it—that he can by no means suppose the Army or any
> part of it in the least endangered by this movement— . . . he
> yet hopes the Event will prove America able to procure that by
> our own Arms which his Allies refuse to assist in Obtaining.[61]

Lafayette bitterly complained against what one of
d'Estaing's officers termed Sullivan's "insolence," [62] and it
seemed to some that the two generals were at the point of a
duel.[63] In response, Sullivan apologized and promised that he
would try to repair some of the damage that his order had
done.[64] To Washington, Lafayette wrote that

> Frenchmen of the highest character have been exposed to the
> most disagreeable circumstances; and yet, myself the friend of
> America, the friend of General Washington, I am more upon a
> warlike footing in the American lines than when I came near
> the British lines at Newport.[65]

For a time it was even rumored that Lafayette intended to return home to France "in disgust in consequence of some inflections cast by Genl Sullivan & others on the French Admiral and in short on all the Nation." [66] Briefly the marquis considered such a move, but as his anger gave way to reason, he rejected it.[67]

On the 26th Sullivan carried out his pledge to the marquis. That day his general orders read:

> It having been supposed by some Persons that by the Orders of the 24th Inst. the Commander in Chief meant to insinuate that the departure of the French Fleet was owing to a fixed determination not to assist in the present enterprise—As the General would not wish to give the least colour for ungenerous and illiberal minds to make such unfair interpretations, he thinks it necessary to say that as he could not determine whether the Removal of the Fleet was absolutely necessary or not and therefore did not mean to censure an act which the Admirals orders might render absolutely necessary—He however hopes that the Speedy return of the Fleet will show their attention and regard to the Alliance formed between us and add to the obligations the Americans are already under to the French nation. However mortifying the Departure of the Fleet was to us at such a time of expectations we ought not too suddenly Censure the movement, or for an act of any kind to forget the aid and Protection which had been offered by the French since the Commencement of the present Contest.[68]

Despite Sullivan's retraction the damage had already been done. Of the order of August 24, Nathanael Greene wrote Washington that "General Sullivan very imprudently issued something like a censure in general orders. Indeed it was an absolute censure. It opened the mouths of the army in very clamorous strains." [69] Greene also informed his chief that "people censure the Admiral with great freedom, and many are impudent enough to reproach the nation through the Admiral." [70] The general's words were an understatement.

Although Sullivan's expression of his wrath had been inadvisable, it was not in itself responsible for the general outburst that followed the French departure from Rhode Island. His actions served far more to deepen and spread the malice that had been born than they did to create it. Before Sullivan ever published his order, considerable sentiment against the French already existed within the American army. Israel Angell, colonel of the 2nd Rhode Island Regiment, noted in his diary on August 23 that "the french . . . left us in a most Rascally manner and what will be the Event God only knows." [71] In this judgment Stephen Olney, a captain in Angell's regiment, concurred. [72] Even the mild-mannered Reverend Manasseh Cutler spoke of the French departure as a "desertion." [73] To his brother in Pennsylvania, Colonel Benjamin Eyre, who was charged with directing a group of ship-carpenters, wrote:

> If the French fleet has a right to fight when they please & Run when they please & leave Gen[l]. Sulavan when they please & his Armey on a small Island where a brittish fleet can surround it when they please which we may expect every hour I do not understand the Alliance made with france twelve hours of their assistance would have put the Enemy compleetly in our possession. We are now here & masters of the field. But to morrow we may be a retreating army. [74]

Samuel Barrett, a friend of Daniel Lyman, penned to General William Heath what was probably one of the most violent reactions:

> What could the worst enemy have done more to deceive and injure us than by the most specious allurements, and under every assurance of support, to draw us into a most critical and hazzardous enterprize and leave us in the very moment of execution, and by withdrawing that support either expose the flower of the New England States to be cut off or their reputation to unmerited censure.
>
> And what must be the feeling of every generous mind on this trying occasion,—if this is Gallic faith we have formed a sweet and hopeful alliance!
>
> Poor Lyman is obliged to read the Female Spectator and any thing he can catch up to keep it out of his thoughts. Do, bless you, says he, call another subject. [75]

In concluding his letter Barrett expressed a sentiment that cast a potentially ominous shadow on the future of Franco-American relations:

> How far general policy will admit these *Heroes of Flight* to be
> treated with the contempt they deserve, I am not able to say,
> but most sincerely shall regret any necessity of Frenchifying in
> our deportment on the occasion.[76]

Civilian comment was no more reserved than was that of
the military. One observer in the Rhode Island area at the
time of the operations stated to a friend:

> The Monsieurs have made a most miserable figure and are
> curs'd by all ranks of people and I believe will be no further
> service than to help Starve us all to the Northward as Provi-
> sions of all kinds have risen amazingly since their arrival at Bos-
> ton.[77]

Of the French efforts to fortify Boston harbor against a possible attack by the British navy, the same writer noted that the
attempt resembled "Baboons cackling." [78]

Dissatisfaction was also evident in the views privately expressed by some congressmen, particularly in the case of the
so-called "radicals" of the New England contingent. To General Horatio Gates, who originally desired command of the expedition, Massachusetts's James Lovell wrote, "I think we
ought to conclude that the Events at Newport will prevent
too much of our Independence being attributed to the Arrival
of the allied-Fleet on our Coasts." [79] More pointed, though
perhaps no less hostile, were the observations which Andrew
Adams of Connecticut passed on to Oliver Wolcott, another
member of his state's delegation:

> . . . I fully agree with you that we are not blindly to trust the
> Justice: much less the Generosity of any Nation unconnected
> with their Interest.
> An Instance on which to ground our Caution I think we have
> before us in the french: fleet leaving R: Island in the midst of an
> Expedition Jointly undertaken and going to Boston in order to
> refit when they might as well refitted there and at the same time
> cooperated with our forces: and also in Carrying off their Land
> as well [as] sea forces. . . .[80]

Writing to Washington, Lafayette urged him to come to
Rhode Island and assume command of the expedition. At the
same time he imparted to his mentor what he termed "the

true reason" for the Americans' chagrin, maintaining that "the leaders of the expedition are, most of them, ashamed to return, after having spoken of their Rhode Island success in proud terms before their family, their friends, their internal enemies." [81] In view of Sullivan's need for a victory to vindicate himself and turn aside the threat to his position which his political enemies had raised, Lafayette's conclusion may not have been far from the mark. With public feeling what it was, the French action gave a perfect excuse for failure, regardless of what effect an attempt to make them scapegoats might have on the alliance, if indeed Sullivan ever considered such an effect.

Notes

1. Sullivan to Henry Laurens, August 10, 1778, in Hammond, ed., *Letters and Papers,* II, 191–92.

2. "Diary of Ezekiel Price," *New England Historical and Genealogical Register,* XIX, 334; James Warren to Elbridge Gerry, August 4, 1778, in C. Harvey Gardiner, ed., *A Study in Dissent: The Warren-Gerry Correspondence, 1776–1792* (Carbondale and Edwardsville: Southern Illinois University Press, 1968), p. 126; Heath, *Memoirs,* p. 202.

3. General Orders and Orderly Book of a Part of the Army under General Sullivan, 1st June–August 25th, 1778, August 10, 1778, RIHS.

4. Heath, *Memoirs,* pp. 202–03; Lyman to Heath, August 11, 1778, in *Heath Papers,* Part II, 246–47.

5. Whittemore, *A General of the Revolution,* p. 94; General Orders and Orderly Book, August 31, 1778, RIHS.

6. Heath to Sullivan, August 8, 1778, in *Heath Papers,* Part II, 245; General Orders and Orderly Book, August 11, 1778, RIHS. Lyman was born in 1756 and graduated from Yale in 1776. In the spring of 1777 he joined Colonel William Lee's regiment and was stationed in Boston for over a year. From May 1778 until the end of the war, he was a member of Heath's staff. *Heath Papers,* Part II, 245.

7. W. C. Watson, *Men and Times of the Revolution: Or Memoirs of Elkanah Watson,* 2nd ed. (n.p., 1856), p. 88; Hiller B. Zobel, *The Boston Massacre* (New York: W. W. Norton, 1970), pp. 147–49 and pp. 340–41, n. 12.

8. Sullivan to Henry Laurens, August 16 [?], 1778, in Hammond, ed., *Letters and Papers,* II, 219–20; Sullivan to Heath, August 11, 1778, in *Ibid.,* p. 197. Although Sullivan's letter to Laurens is dated August 16 by Hammond, it manifestly was written sometime after August 20, as it refers to d'Estaing's departure for Boston. The French did not even return to Rhode Island until August 20.

9. Moré, *Pontgibaud,* pp. 66–67.

10. Sullivan to Washington, August 13, 1778, in Hammond, ed., *Letters and Papers,* II, 205–06; Sullivan to Governor William Greene, August 12, 1778, in *Ibid.,* pp. 199–200; Cutler and Perkins, *Manasseh Cutler,* I, 66–67; "Part of a Diary of Major Gibbs, 1778," *Pennsylvania Archives,* VI (1853), 734–35; Jabez Bowen to Governor Greene, August 13, 1778, Letters to the Governors of Rhode Island, R.I. State Archives.

11. Mackenzie, *Diary,* II, 349–52; Popp, *Diary of Stephan Popp,* p. 12.

12. Sullivan to Washington, August 13, 1778, in Hammond, ed., *Letters and Papers,* II, 206.

13. Theodore Thayer, *Nathanael Greene: Strategist of the American Revolution* (New York: Twayne Publishers, 1960), p. 254.

14. Mackenzie, *Diary,* II, 350.

15. Sullivan to Washington, August 13, 1778, in Hammond, ed., *Letters and Papers,* II, 205–07; Sullivan to Henry Laurens, August 14, 1778, in *Ibid.,* pp. 212–14.

16. Sullivan to Governor Greene, August 13, 1778, in Hammond, ed., *Letters and Papers,* II, 203–04.

17. General Orders and Orderly Book, August 14, 1778, RIHS.

18. General Orders and Orderly Book, August 10 and 14, 1778, RIHS; Cutler and Perkins, *Manasseh Cutler,* I, 67–68; Lyman to Heath, August 15, 1778, in *Heath Papers,* Part II, 252; Noah Robinson, Journal, RIHS; Edwin M. Stone, *The Life and Recollections of John Howland* (Providence: George H. Whitney, 1857), p. 94.

19. J. M. Greene to [?], August 19, 1778, RIHS MSS, VI, 112.

20. Cutler and Perkins, *Manasseh Cutler,* I, 67–68; Mackenzie, *Diary,* II, 353; John Laurens to Henry Laurens, August 22, 1778, in Laurens, *Army Correspondence,* p. 220.

21. Council of War at Providence, July 25, 1778, in Hammond, ed., *Letters and Papers,* II, 114; Cullum, *Fortification Defenses,* p. 14.

22. Cullum, *Fortification Defenses,* p. 14.

23. *Ibid.* Cullum's conclusions have been supplemented by personal inspection of the terrain.

24. John Laurens to Henry Laurens, August 22, 1778, in Laurens, *Army Correspondence,* pp. 220–21.

25. Cutler and Perkins, *Manasseh Cutler,* I, 69.

26. Willcox, *Portrait of a General,* pp. 246–47.

27. Paul Revere to his wife, August [?], 1778, in *Massachusetts Historical Society Proceedings,* XIII (February 1874), 251.

28. Sullivan to Governor Greene, August 15, 1778, in Hammond, ed., *Letters and Papers,* II, 214–15; Sullivan to the New Hampshire Council, August 16, 1778, in *Ibid.,* 224–26.

29. Governor Greene to Sullivan, August 19, 1778, in *Ibid.,* p. 231; Massachusetts Council to Sullivan, August 19, 1778, in *Ibid.,* p. 236.

30. Governor Greene to Sullivan, August 17, 1778, in Hammond, ed., *Letters and Papers,* II, 226–27; Sullivan to Governor Greene, August 18, 1778, in *Ibid.,* pp. 229–30; State of Rhode Island and Providence Plantations, Council of War, August 17, 1778, printed broadside, Broadside File, RIHS.

31. Sullivan to Governor Greene, August 19, 1778, in Hammond, ed., *Letters and Papers*, II, 232.

32. Lyman to Heath, August 19, 1778, *Heath Papers,* Part II, 256; Pigot to Clinton, August 31, 1778, in *Rhode Island Historical Tracts,* No. 6, p. 87.

33. Mackenzie, *Diary,* II, 358–59.

34. Mackenzie, *Diary,* II, 347, 351–52, 355; Pigot to Clinton, August 31, 1778, in *Rhode Island Historical Tracts,* No. 6, p. 86.

35. Mackenzie, *Diary,* II, 361; Pigot to Clinton, August 31, 1778, in *Rhode Island Historical Tracts,* No. 6, p. 87; Samuel Ward, Jr., to Phebe Ward, August 20, 1778, Ward MSS, RIHS; "Diary of Major Gibbs," *Pennsylvania Archives,* VI, 735; Cutler and Perkins, *Manasseh Cutler,* I, 70.

36. "Diary of Major Gibbs," *Pennsylvania Archives,* VI, 735; Thomas Crafts to William Heath, April 21, 1778, in *Heath Papers,* Part II, 256–57; Mackenzie, *Diary,* II, 363–64; Almy, "Journal," *Newport Historical Magazine,* I, 32–33.

37. Nathanael Greene to John Brown, September 6, 1778, in Greene, *Life of Greene,* II, 134; Cutler and Perkins, *Manasseh Cutler,* I, 70–71.

38. Cutler and Perkins, *Manasseh Cutler,* I, 71.

39. Count de Cambis to Sullivan, August 20, 1778, in Hammond, ed., *Letters and Papers,* II, 237–38; d'Estaing to Sullivan, August 21, 1778, in *Ibid.,* pp. 240–42. The theme of Sullivan's message may be inferred by d'Estaing's answer of the 21st. Sullivan to Henry Laurens, August 16 [?], 1778, in *Ibid.,* p. 219. The text of this letter makes it clear that Hammond misdated it, for it refers specifically to d'Estaing's departure for Boston.

40. D'Estaing to Sullivan, September 8, 1778, in Comte d'Estaing and George Washington, *Washington, sa Correspondance avec d'Estaing* (Paris: Publié par les Soins de la Fondation Nationale pour la Reproduction des Manuscrits Précieux et Pièces Rares d'Archives, 1937), p. 9.

41. Greene, *Life of Greene,* II, 116–18; Nathanael Greene to Charles Pettit, August 22, 1778, in *Ibid.,* pp. 119–20; "Diary of Major Gibbs," *Pennsylvania Archives,* VI, 735; d'Estaing to Sullivan, August 21, 1778, in Hammond, ed., *Letters and Papers,* II, 242; Lafayette to Washington, August 25, in Sparks, ed., *Letters to Washington,* II, 184; John Laurens to Henry Laurens, August 22, 1778, in Laurens, *Army Correspondence,* p. 221; John Laurens to Washington, August 23, 1778, in Sparks, ed., *Letters to Washington,* II, 180–81.

42. John Laurens to Washington, in Sparks, ed., *Letters to Washington,* II, 180.

43. Greene, *Life of Greene,* II, 117–18; Freeman, *Washington,* V, 68; Sullivan to Washington, August 23, 1778, in Hammond, ed., *Letters and Papers,* II, 264.

44. Henry Laurens to Sullivan, August 28, 1778, in Burnett, ed., *Letters of Members of the Continental Congress,* III, 338.

45. Sullivan to Washington, August 23, 1778, in Hammond, ed., *Letters and Papers,* II, 264. Sullivan's letter does not appear in Hammond, but its tone may be inferred from d'Estaing's response on August 30, 1778, in *Ibid.,* pp. 277–78, and from a letter sent by d'Estaing to Nathanael Greene on October 1, in Greene, *Life of Greene,* II, 148–49.

46. Mackenzie, *Diary,* II, 367.

47. Sullivan to Washington, August 23, 1778, in Hammond, ed., *Letters and Papers,* II, 264; Lafayette to Washington, August 25, 1778, in Sparks, ed., *Letters to Washington,* II, 184; David Ramsay, *The History of the American Revolution,* 2 vols. (London: printed for John Stockdale, 1793), p. 90.

48. General Sullivan and his officers to the Count d'Estaing, August 22, 1778, in Hammond, ed., *Letters and Papers,* II, 245.

49. *Ibid.,* 246.

50. Lafayette to Washington, August 25, 1778, in Sparks, ed., *Letters to Washington,* II, 184; Stephenson and Dunn, *Washington,* II, 99; Gottschalk, *Lafayette,* II, 255.

51. Lafayette to d'Estaing, August 22, 1778, in Doniol, *Histoire,* VI, 420.

52. John Laurens to Henry Laurens, August 22, 1778, in Laurens, *Army Correspondence,* p. 221; John Laurens to Washington, August 23, 1778, in Sparks, ed., *Letters to Washington,* II, 179–80; Gottschalk, *Lafayette,* II, 256.

53. "Diary of Major Gibbs," *Pennsylvania Archives,* VI, 735; Mackenzie, *Diary,* II, 368–69.

54. Nathanael Greene to Sullivan, August 23, 1778, in Hammond, ed., *Letters and Papers,* II, 252.

55. Nathanael Greene to Washington, August 28, 1778, in Greene, *Life of Greene,* II, 125.

56. General Orders and Orderly Book, August 24, 1778, RIHS.

57. Samuel Ward, Jr., to Phebe Ward, August 24, 1778, Ward MSS, RIHS. Ward was the son of Rhode Island's Governor Samuel Ward, and had served in virtually every major operation of the army since the siege of Boston, including Arnold's march to Quebec.

58. Nathanael Greene to Washington, August 28, 1778, in Greene, *Life of Greene,* II, 126; "Diary of Ezekiel Price," *New England Historical and Genealogical Register,* XIX, 336.

59. Lafayette to d'Estaing, August 24, 1778, in Doniol, *Histoire,* VI, 425–26.

60. Lafayette to d'Estaing, August 24, 1778, in *Ibid.,* pp. 422–23.

61. General Orders, August 24, 1778, in Hammond, ed., *Letters and Papers,* III, 644–45; General Orders and Orderly Book, August 24, 1778, RIHS.

62. *Extrait de journal,* p. 25.

63. Moré, *Pontgibaud,* p. 68.

64. Lafayette to Washington, August 25, 1778, in Sparks, ed., *Letters to Washington,* II, 185.

65. Lafayette to Washington, August 25, 1778, in Sparks, ed., *Letters to Washington,* II, 185.

66. William Stewart to William Goddard, September 10, 1778, Military Papers, V, 35, RIHS.

67. Gottschalk, *Lafayette,* II, 259.

68. General Orders and Orderly Book, August 26, 1778, RIHS.

69. Nathanael Greene to Washington, August 28, 1778, in Greene, *Life of Greene,* II, 127.

70. *Ibid.*

71. Israel Angell, *The Diary of Israel Angell,* ed. by Edward Field (Providence: Preston & Rounds Co., 1899), p. 4.

72. Captain Stephen Olney's Account of that part of the Revolutionary

War in which he took part . . . , p. 18, Olney Papers, RIHS; Williams, *Biography of Revolutionary Heroes,* p. 251.

73. Cutler and Perkins, *Manasseh Cutler,* I, 71.

74. Benjamin Eyre to Colonel John Eyre, August 24, 1778, in "Original Letters and Documents," *Pennsylvania Magazine of History and Biography,* V (1881), 477.

75. Samuel Barrett to Heath, August 23, 1778, in *Heath Papers,* Part II, 259.

76. Barrett to Heath, August 23, 1778, in *Heath Papers,* Part II, 260.

77. William Stewart to William Goddard, September 10, 1778, Military Papers, V, 35, RIHS.

78. *Ibid.*

79. James Lovell to Horatio Gates, September 18, 1778, in Burnett, ed., *Letters of Members of Congress,* III, 418.

80. Andrew Adams to Oliver Wolcott, August 29, 1778, in Burnett, ed., *Letters of Members of Congress,* III, 391.

81. Lafayette to Washington, August 25, 1778, in Sparks, ed., *Letters to Washington,* II, 186.

VIII

The Battle of Rhode Island

ON THE CLEAR, STILL EVENING of August 20, while the Allies deliberated over whether the French fleet should remain at Rhode Island, Lieutenant Stanhope, one of Brisbaine's officers, and six sailors pushed off from Easton's Beach in a whaleboat bound for New York with word of d'Estaing's return. Skirting the eastern shore of Long Island to avoid any French vessels lurking near the Sound, and pushing through heavy seas which threatened to sink his tiny craft, Stanhope reached his destination on the morning of the 24th and delivered Pigot's call for aid. The day before, the *Galatea*, which on August 18 Howe had sent in company with the *Ariel* and *Experiment* to cruise in search of the French, had returned with a report that it had seen d'Estaing's ships anchored off Newport on the same evening that Stanhope set out on his voyage. With Stanhope's arrival Howe led most of his ships out over the bar, and on August 25, with the rest of his fleet across Sandy Hook, he set sail for Rhode Island. Clinton remained behind, still preparing his transports and moving his men to their embarkation points.[1]

En route to Narragansett Bay, in hope of once again drawing the French off for a naval battle, Howe was met by the *Galatea*, which had been sent ahead to contact Pigot. From her the admiral learned of d'Estaing's departure. Guessing the

Frenchman's destination, Howe set a course for Boston in hope of cutting the enemy fleet off before it could arrive. Failing in this, he arrived off Boston on August 30, two days behind the French. During that time the French had managed to throw up some fortifications to guard Nantasket Roads, and Howe deemed it impracticable to launch an attack.[2]

While Stanhope made his way to New York, Sullivan's strength continued to dwindle daily, and the American commander felt compelled on August 23 to turn to his generals for advice on the army's future course of action. General John Glover proposed that the siege be continued in the same manner, but he pointed out that if this were done the forts at the northern end of the island and the ferries to the mainland should be secured, lest the arrival of British reinforcements necessitate a withdrawal. Glover's proposal was supported by most of his fellow officers. Nathanael Greene thought that an assault on the British line with the number of men the Americans still had would be disastrous. Instead, he and Glover proposed a scheme that John Laurens also strongly favored. In their view, a force of three hundred men in small boats, led by Laurens, would land near the right flank of the British lines and carry the redoubt guarding Easton's Beach at the point of the bayonet. With this accomplished, the main portion of the army would file across the beach and form on the heights to the south of the town, thus taking the British in the rear. To divert the enemy's attention, feint attacks by the remainder of the militia would be made along the outer line from Tomini Hill to the American position at Honeyman's. The proposal died aborning when it was decided the army did not have enough men to carry out the necessary maneuvers.[3]

On the evening of August 24 Sullivan received a dispatch from Washington warning him that the enemy was assembling over a hundred vessels in Long Island Sound, which might well be intended to transport a relief expedition to Newport. That same night Sullivan called a council of war, during which it was decided that the army should withdraw to

From Washington Irving, *Life of George Washington*, II, 386

BRIGADIER GENERAL JOHN GLOVER

the forts at the north of the island where its position would be more secure and it could await the return of d'Estaing's fleet.[4] The generals' lingering hopes of assistance were not without foundation, for before leaving for Boston d'Estaing had told Lafayette that if he could quickly obtain the masts he needed to repair his ships, "three weeks after my arrival I shall go out again, and then we shall fight for the glory of the French name, and the interests of America."[5] Indeed, on the 23rd Sullivan had attempted to raise the spirits of his men by assuring them in his general orders that the French would soon sail to their aid, although Major Ward probably expressed the feelings of the men toward such a prospect when he commented that "we all have our *Doubts*."[6]

Earlier in the day Sullivan had already made the preliminary preparations for his retreat by sending two hundred men to the north of the island. There they were to assist the troops who had been left behind when the army marched south in erecting new fortifications under the direction of Colonels Evans and Gidley. At the same time, all of the guns which could be spared from the siege lines were to be removed to the north. In addition, the company of Salem volunteers was ordered to march to Howland's Ferry and place itself under the command of Colonel Richard Lee, in order to man the boats, as it was ominously phrased, "when occasion may require."[7] That night, with the retreat determined upon, the guns and mortars on the lower part of Honeyman's Hill were withdrawn, and news of the council's decision spread throughout the army.[8]

While Sullivan prepared to fall back, he continued to make urgent appeals to the New England states for reinforcements in the hope that by strengthening his army he would be able to maintain his hold on the north until the French could return.[9] By this time the total number of Rhode Island's militiamen left on the mainland amounted to some sixty men, most of them invalids, who were guarding Providence.[10] In answer to the general's appeal, Governor William Greene, at the behest of the Council of War, informed Sullivan that the state would be unable to leave its militia on the island after the men's term of duty expired.[11] In a second letter, written in much the same vein, Governor Greene gave as the state's reason the fact that "some Guards are necessary for our extensive Shores having on them a most valuable Stock with large quantities of Cheese and the people being in danger of being taken out of their Beds by small Parties." The Governor then generously suggested that Sullivan seek his reinforcements "from the neighbouring States."[12]

On August 25 the British bombarded Sullivan's works for an hour and a half. In return, the Americans fired only a few shots with their remaining guns, and while they strengthened their fortifications they ceased their efforts to push their parallels toward the enemy lines. The next day the two sides engaged in an even more feeble cannonade. Having observed that Sullivan had discontinued his approaches, Pigot's suspicion that his enemy intended to retreat was strengthened when an American deserter informed the British that Sullivan planned to move to the north. In an effort to gain more positive intelligence, Pigot sent out reconnaissance patrols on the night of the 26th, but their prisoners gave conflicting testimony and he could not be certain whether Sullivan intended to withdraw or make an attempt to storm the British position.[13] While Pigot attempted to fathom the Americans' intentions, Sullivan called another officers' council, at which it was concluded that the army should continue to hold its position on Honeyman's Hill until it could be reinforced.[14]

By 2:00 P.M. on August 27 three of Howe's frigates, the *Sphynx* and the *Vigilant* (both 20 guns) and the *Nautilus* (16 guns), anchored in Newport's harbor. In greeting, three cheers went up along the British line, a display of joy that did not go unnoticed by the Americans. From the ships Pigot learned that Howe was on his way to Boston, but he was assured by Colonel Stuart, who had sailed with Howe, that reinforcements could be expected from Clinton momentarily.[15]

On the same day that Howe's detachment reached Newport, Clinton, with four thousand troops, finally sailed to the relief of the town's garrison. Sir Henry's plan involved more than lifting the siege, for he hoped to run up Narragansett Passage and interdict Sullivan's line of retreat to the mainland by seizing Bristol Neck and blocking Howland's Ferry with his warships. Sullivan's army would then be trapped on Rhode Island and could be either captured or destroyed. With Sullivan disposed of, Clinton could then move against Providence. The weather, however, delayed Clinton's progress, and for three days his ships had to sail against contrary winds.[16]

On the evening of the 27th, following another council, Lafayette, at the request of his fellow officers, who had long been urging him to go, left for Boston in order to determine what d'Estaing's intentions were. Riding all that night, Lafayette covered the seventy miles to Boston in only seven hours.[17]

Finally, on August 28, with the army's stores and heavy baggage already removed to the north, the council decided to fall back on the northern fortifications. That night at eight o'clock the troops broke camp. An hour later they were given the order to march, with Greene and the right wing taking the West Road, and the left wing—now commanded by Glover— the second line, the reserve, and the artillery moving by the East Road. At 10:00 P.M. the advanced guard began its withdrawal, and two hours later the advanced pickets, who had been left facing Pigot's line, were drawn off. Between 2:00 A.M. and 3:00 A.M. the troops reached the area of Butts Hill and occupied the line of works. There they pitched their tents.

Thus Sullivan's army, now numbering between five thousand and six thousand men, formed a defensive line facing Newport, the line stretching from the eastern to the western shore of the island. Deployed in front of the intrenchments was the first line. On the left, with Quaker Hill looming to his front, was Glover. In the center, with Butts Hill Fort to the rear, was Colonel Christopher Greene, temporarily detached from command of his regiment in order to lead a brigade. To

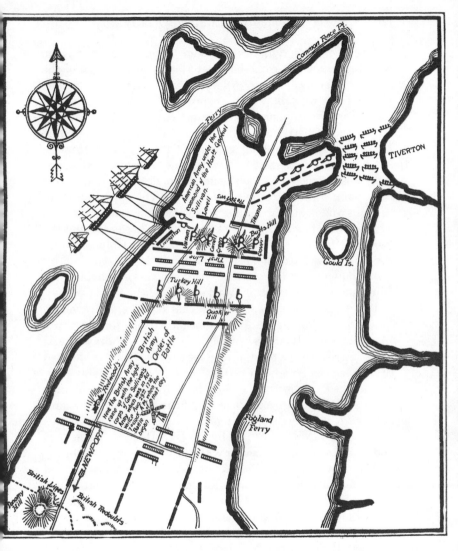

MAP OF THE BATTLE OF RHODE ISLAND

Colonel Greene's right was Ezekiel Cornell, whose brigade rested its right flank on the West Road. On the right of the road and facing Turkey Hill was James Varnum's brigade. Holding the redoubt which anchored the right wing on the shore was Christopher Greene's regiment (actually not much larger than a battalion), which included about one hundred Blacks, now led by Major Samuel Ward, Jr. Protecting the left flank was General Tyler, while the task of guarding the right was entrusted to Lieutenant Colonel Henry Brockholst Livingston. Posted to the southward, on the opposite side of the hills and some three miles in front of the army, were two advanced parties serving as skirmishers. Those blocking the West Road were under Colonel Laurens, while Colonel Henry Beekman Livingston held the East Road.[18]

As dawn cast its orange-red streaks of light over Honeyman's Hill, Captain Mackenzie saw the empty American works and the large open area that had been the enemy's campsite. Galloping to Pigot's headquarters in the town, Mackenzie informed his chief of Sullivan's withdrawal, and Pigot hurried to the outer line in his cariole. There he decided to hamper the American retreat. At 6:30 A.M. General Prescott moved out with the 38th and 54th Regiments over Easton's Beach to occupy the fortifications on Honeyman's Hill. At the same time, Brigadier General Francis Smith marched toward Quaker Hill by the East Road with the 22nd and 33rd Regiments, together with the flank companies of the 38th and 54th. On the West Road Captain von Malsberg and Captain Noltenius, each with his company of Hessian Chasseurs, advanced toward Laurens. Behind these two companies came Major General von Lossberg leading the two Anspach battalions.[19]

At seven o'clock von Malsberg spotted Laurens and Talbot with the Light Corps posted behind some stone walls to the south of the Redwood House. Drawing in his advanced guard, the German formed his men, went forward with a rush towards the American skirmishers, and drove them back towards Laurens's main body. On the East Road things went differently. Overconfident, Smith failed to send out flanking parties or an advance guard. Moments after von Malsberg launched his charge on the west, Smith paid for his folly. As his troops approached the windmill near Quaker Hill, Livingston's men sprang up behind a stone wall and a crashing volley of musketry ripped through the British ranks, taking a heavy toll.[20]

Hearing the crackle of gunfire on the West Road, Pigot soon received a report that Smith was opposed by large numbers of the enemy on his front. Immediately the British general ordered von Huyne's Regiment and Fanning's Regiment of Provincials to von Lossberg's support. At the same time, Pigot sent word to Prescott to dispatch the 54th Regiment to reinforce Smith, and Brown's Regiment marched out of the lines to Smith's aid. Lest the American retreat and the engagements to the north prove a ruse to draw his army away from the town, Pigot remained in the British lines with the Landgrave, Ditfourth, and Bunau Regiments, prepared to check a possible assault.[21]

By 7:30 von Lossberg had marched out of the lines with the main body of his column, and an hour later he came to the Chausseurs' aid. Slowly Laurens and his men fell back. Then, before the combined attack of von Lossberg and the two regiments that had reinforced him, the Light Corps was forced to retreat across Lawton's Valley to the works on a small height in front of Turkey Hill. Shifting his men to the right, von Malsberg enabled his general's column to storm the hillock from three sides. With a cheer, the Germans and Fanning's corps charged up the slope in the face of a single, poorly aimed volley and cleared the top with the bayonet. Forced to retreat to Turkey Hill, Laurens was able to fall back on the regiment that Sullivan had sent to reinforce him, and which had already taken post on the hill's summit. With these men came the stipulation that Laurens and his force retire to the main army in the best possible order.

Quickly von Lossberg renewed his assault and drove the Americans from Turkey Hill as well. Halting in their retreat, a small American detachment deployed in a cornfield. As the enemy troops rushed by, with Noltenius's Chasseurs on the extreme right, the concealed Americans let loose a volley that enfiladed Noltenius's advancing line and sent the Hessian captain sprawling on the ground with a musket ball in him. When von Malsberg turned his men and rushed to the aid of his wounded comrade, the Americans made good their escape.

All the while, even as he continued to retire back toward Sullivan's line, Laurens galloped about, his sword flashing, as he ordered his men to take cover behind walls and thickets, readying them to receive another charge. It came with a vengeance as the enemy flanked both wings and drove for the center, sending the Americans scurrying to yet another improvised line. Continuing to drive the rebels before them, von Lossberg's units pursued Laurens's men to the verges of Nathanael Greene's wing of the army. There von Lossberg halted, and the main body of his troops retired behind the southern slope of Turkey Hill, safe from the American cannon shot. While von Lossberg's guns on the hill's summit commenced a cannonade of the American lines, his infantrymen refreshed themselves, renewed their ammunition, and waited.[22]

Recovering from Livingston's ambush, the flank companies of Smith's column quickly fanned out from the road, while the 22nd and 43rd Regiments pressed on through galling American fire. To support Livingston, Sullivan sent another regiment with a warning similar to that directed to Laurens. On Livingston's front the battle raged fiercely. Before the struggle ended, Major Tousard, a member of Lafayette's military family, had his horse blown out from under him and his right arm severed while leading a charge against a British artillery piece.

Continually retiring back toward the army's main line while putting up a stout resistance, the Americans climbed to the summit of Quaker Hill, and there, for a moment, disaster threatened them. From the West Road a German regiment angled off and marched toward Livingston's position. With Livingston already outflanked by von Lossberg's successful assault on Turkey Hill, the advancing German regiment appeared intent on linking up with Smith and cutting off the retreat of Colonel Edward Wigglesworth and his regiment, now holding a key position on the top of Quaker Hill. To warn Wigglesworth, Sullivan sent one of his volunteer aides, Colonel John Trumbull.[23] Galloping up to the crest of Quaker Hill, with musket balls whizzing by him and grapeshot sprinkling around his path, Trumbull reached Wigglesworth's line. Reluctantly Wigglesworth obeyed Sullivan's order and began to draw off his men. Then, before the reinforcements Pigot had sent him could come up, Smith launched a charge that sent Livingston's men pouring down the hill with the British in close pursuit.

Sweeping up another regiment which Sullivan had sent to their support, the retreating Americans ran towards Glover's line, where they took refuge. As Smith's troops rushed at the American defenses, Glover steadied his men and met the British charge with massed musketry and artillery fire. In the forefront of the fight, Lieutenant Colonel Campbell of the 22nd Regiment saw his nephew cut down by his side. Forced to retreat, Campbell reluctantly left the boy's body on the field and with the rest of Smith's men fell back across the mile-wide valley between Butts Hill and the British position on Quaker and Turkey Hills. Seeing the strength of the American position, Smith decided against launching a major assault, and from Quaker and Turkey Hills the British began a bombardment of Glover's sector at about 9:00 A.M., but failed to dislodge the troops there.[24]

During the lull between attacks the cannonade and skirmishing between the advanced parties of both armies continued.[25] While the stage was being set for the battle's second act, events behind the British lines took on an ugly character.

As von Lossberg's Germans advanced across Lawton's Valley, stragglers from his column proceeded to rob the inhabitants and murder at least one of them.[26] While this was taking place, Pigot was having difficulty with his ill-tempered second in command. When Prescott received Pigot's order to send the 54th Regiment to Smith's support, he had returned to the outer line with the 38th and made a display of his anger with Pigot for not sending him to take command of Smith's column during the battle. Prescott then dashed off a letter to his commander in which he accused Pigot of ill-treating him in this respect. Pigot tried to explain that if he had allowed Prescott to supersede either Smith or von Lossberg, he would be casting doubt on their abilities. Prescott, however, continued to fume.[27]

Refusing a request by Nathanael Greene to bring on a general action by attacking the enemy position, Sullivan held to his resolve to remain where he was and beat off the enemy's assaults. He had not long to wait. As soon as the two enemy columns had marched out of the British lines in pursuit of Sullivan's army, the *Sphynx,* the *Vigilant,* the *Spitfire Galley,* and a privateer brig that had recently arrived got underway and stood to the north. By ten o'clock the four ships had worked their way into the passage between Rhode Island and Prudence, where they could bombard the right flank of the American battle line. With the vessels to support him, von Lossberg ordered his men to charge, and they made an attempt to turn the American right flank by taking the advanced redoubt held by Major Ward and the newly raised "Colored Regiment." There the German general's troops met a stubborn defense and were compelled to fall back. Reforming their line, they advanced again, bayoneting the American wounded as they came, but were thrown back once more. Challenged by two twenty-four-pounders in the redoubt on the tip of Bristol Neck and by two eighteen-pounders which General Greene's men ran down to the beach near Ward's position, the four British ships bombarded the American posi-

tion with two or three broadsides and then dropped down the
channel to anchor opposite the British position.[28]

At 2:00 P.M. von Lossberg launched his heaviest assault
against General Greene's wing of the army. Even in the face
of four regiments which Greene deployed to reinforce the
threatened sector of his front, the enemy continued to advance until they were some one hundred yards in the rear of
Ward's redoubt. Quickly Greene led a counterattack with two
regiments. One of these was Colonel Israel Angell's 2nd Rhode
Island Regiment, the other General James Lovell's brigade of
Massachusetts militia that Sullivan had ordered Trumbull to
bring from the second line to the support of the embattled
Greene.[29] In addition Sullivan sent forward Colonel Henry
Brockholst Livingston's Light Corps. With a swirling flash of
bayonets the Americans drove von Lossberg's troops back
from the endangered redoubt.

As the American counterattack continued to swell to some
fifteen hundred men, Greene's troops attempted to turn von
Lossberg's right flank. To meet the crisis, von Malsberg deployed his Chasseurs behind a stone wall and disputed the
American advance until he was in danger of being over-
whelmed. Unable to stand against the Americans' superior
numbers, von Lossberg's troops fell back in some confusion to
the summit of Turkey Hill, although some of them, including
von Malsberg, fought back as best they could. By three
o'clock the attack was over, and some of the Americans were
holding a position behind a stone wall some three hundred
paces from Turkey Hill.[30] In Nathanael Greene's words, "we
soon put the enemy to the rout, and I had the pleasure to see
them run in worse disorder than they did at the battle of
Monmouth." [31]

Elated by his success in beating back the enemy's attacks,
Sullivan considered making his victory complete by launching
an assault against the British positions on Quaker and Turkey
Hills, but prudently decided against such an action. His men
had neither eaten nor slept since his abandonment of the siege

lines before Newport. In addition, the enemy held a strong position studded with twenty pieces of artillery, and an assault would expose him to their fire as he crossed the large open valley between Butts Hill and the British-held slopes.[32]

At 2:00 P.M. Pigot arrived at Quaker Hill to observe the action. Two hours later he sent orders to Newport for the Landgrave and Ditfourth Regiments to march to von Lossberg's support, and they arrived near seven o'clock.[33]

Towards evening an attempt was made to cut off and surround the Hessian Chasseurs who held an exposed position on the British left. When the firing began, the von Huyne Regiment and Fanning's detachment reinforced the Chasseurs, and following a sharp engagement the Americans retreated.[34] The battle at length came to a close with continued skirmishing and a cannonade that lasted until nightfall.[35] Sullivan's casualties were 30 dead, 137 wounded, and 44 missing.[36] Pigot had 38 killed, 210 wounded, and 44 missing. Of his casualties, 128 were German.[37] In all, one-fifth of the total number of men engaged in the fighting were casualties, a relatively high rate in terms of eighteenth century warfare.[38] Pigot's casualty return included one of his men who was taken prisoner on John Glover's front. As Sergeant Ebenezer Wild of Colonel Joseph Vose's 1st Massachusetts Regiment matter-of-factly put it, "we took one prisoner in the action which deserted from our side when Fort Mungunnery [Montgomery] was besieged by the enemy. We shot him in about an hour after we took him prisoner." [39]

On August 30 the two armies remained in their positions, exchanging artillery fire and an occasional musket shot. That day Sullivan received a letter from Boston informing him that d'Estaing would not be able to sail for some time. In another letter the general learned from Washington that Lord Howe's fleet had sailed from New York, and at the same time word reached him of a fleet lying at anchor off Block Island. Immediately Sullivan called a council of war, and it was decided that the army should retreat back to Tiverton and its base at Fort Barton. Throughout the day the army moved its supplies and baggage across to the mainland, while Sullivan had redoubts constructed and tents pitched in sight of the British to cover his intentions. Yet they were not so easily deceived, for the removal of the supplies and equipment attracted their attention, and they were further enlightened by an American deserter.[40]

That same day in his general orders Sullivan squelched an ugly rumor that Ward's "colored" troops had failed to do their duty in the battle of the previous day. Unequivocally he stated that "upon inquiry from Major Ward & Sundry other officers who were with them in action—there is not the lest foundation for sensure." [41] In point of fact, Christopher Greene's regiment had lost two dead, nine wounded, and eleven missing.[42]

At 6:00 P.M. Sullivan gave the order to retreat from the island. Two hours later the men were marching for Howland's Ferry. While the retreat was in progress, near eleven o'clock, Lafayette returned from his fruitless mission to Boston with the report that d'Estaing's fleet would not return. The marquis, chagrined at missing the battle, then took command of the pickets covering the withdrawal and was among the last to leave the island. Crossing under the cover of the guns of Fort Barton at Tiverton and the "Owl's Nest" on Gould Island, the main part of the army reached Tiverton shortly before midnight. Three hours later the last of the Americans also made good their escape.[43]

Sullivan's evacuation would not have been peaceful or so easy had it not been for the doubts of Major General Prescott. With Pigot falling ill on August 30, Prescott had come to Quaker Hill to take command of the advanced position. As the Americans crossed the East Passage, Prescott was informed at 10:00 P.M. that the sound of the rebels' boats and a number of voices had been heard in the channel. Although Prescott considered attacking the retreating army and taking it in the rear, he declined to act, for he had received no orders to move against Sullivan's force should it retreat, and the ground which he had to assault would have been unfavorable to him. In the end, still fuming over Pigot's conduct toward him the day of the battle, Prescott refused to risk failure and possible censure.[44]

On September 1 Clinton, whose ships had anchored off Block Island on August 30, landed at Newport, too late to catch his quarry. Sir Henry's arrival, however, did not bring Pigot either praise or reward for his successful defense of the island. Instead, Clinton was disappointed by Sullivan's escape, and his temper turned foul as it often could. He criticized his subordinate for attacking the enemy on the 29th rather than waiting for reinforcements to arrive, and for remaining on the field during the night instead of returning to the lines around Newport. In Clinton's view, Pigot had risked a possible successful American counterattack and the loss of the island.[45]

Clinton and his fleet sailed from Newport on September 2, and the next day he headed for New York, leaving his troops and ships under command of General Charles Grey, of "Paoli Massacre" fame, with instructions to raid the New England coast.[46] On September 6 Grey raided New Bedford and Fairhaven in Massachusetts. There he captured Fort Phoenix, which guarded the entrance to the Acushnet River. In eighteen hours Grey destroyed approximately one hundred ships, most of which were privateers, and burned nearly forty warehouses filled with produce and naval stores. From here Grey sailed to Martha's Vineyard where, on September 10–11, he destroyed a number of boats and a salt work, confiscated the inhabitants' arms, and seized three hundred oxen and ten thousand sheep. Thus Grey's torches brought to a close the campaign that Sullivan and the Americans had begun so hopefully just a little over a month before.[47]

Notes

1. Mackenzie, *Diary*, II, 365; O'Beirne, *The Fleet under Lord Howe*, pp. 37–39; John André, *Major André's Journal: Operations of the British Army under Lieutenant Generals Sir William Howe and Sir Henry Clinton, June 1777 to November 1778* (Tarrytown: William Abbott, 1930), pp. 83–85.

2. O'Beirne, *The Fleet under Lord Howe,* pp. 39–40; Gruber, "Richard Lord Howe," in Billias, ed., *Washington's Opponents,* p. 351; Heath, *Memoirs,* p. 205.

3. John Glover to Sullivan, August 23, 1778, in Hammond, ed., *Letters and Papers,* II, 261–62; Nathanael Greene to Sullivan, August 23, 1778, in *Ibid.,* pp. 250–54; Nathanael Greene to Washington, August 28, 1778, in Greene, *Life of Greene,* II, 125–26.

4. Washington to Sullivan, August 22, 1778, in Fitzpatrick, ed., *Writings of Washington,* XII, 350; Whittemore, *A General of the Revolution,* p. 104; Lafayette to d'Estaing, August 24, 1778, in Doniol, *Histoire,* VI, 256.

5. Lafayette to Washington, August 25, 1778, in Sparks, ed., *Letters to Washington,* II, 184.

6. Samuel Ward, Jr., to Phebe Ward, August 24, 1778, Ward MSS, RIHS.

7. General Orders and Orderly Book, August 24, 1778, RIHS; Book of General Orders Belonging to the Adjutant of Colonel Christopher Greene's Regiment, 1778, August 24, 1778, RIHS.

8. Angell, *Diary of Israel Angell,* p. 5; Noah Robinson, Journal, RIHS.

9. Sullivan to the New Hampshire Committee of Safety, August 26, 1778, in Hammond, ed., *Letters and Papers,* II, 269.

10. Governor William Greene to Jonathan Trumbull, August 25, 1778, in *The Trumbull Papers, Massachusetts Historical Society Collections,* 7th series, Vol. III, Part IV (Boston: Massachusetts Historical Society, 1902), 254.

11. William Greene to Sullivan, August 24, 1778, in Hammond, ed., *Letters and Papers,* II, 265–66.

12. William Greene to Sullivan, August 26, 1778, in Hammond, ed., *Letters and Papers,* II, 273.

13. Mackenzie, *Diary,* II, 372–74; Pigot to Clinton, August 31, 1778, in *Rhode Island Historical Tracts,* No. 6, pp. 87–89.

14. Sullivan to Washington, August 29, 1778, in Hammond, ed., *Letters and Papers,* II, 275; "Diary of Major Gibbs," *Pennsylvania Archives,* VI, 736; Samuel Ward, Jr., to Phebe Ward, August 28, 1778, Ward MSS, RIHS.

15. Mackenzie, *Diary,* II, 376; Pigot to Clinton, August 31, 1778, in *Rhode Island Historical Tracts,* No. 6, p. 89; Samuel Ward, Jr., to Phebe Ward, August 28, 1778, Ward MSS, RIHS.

16. Clinton, *American Rebellion,* pp. 102–03; André, *Major André's Journal,* pp. 84–86.

17. Sullivan to the President of Congress, August 31, 1778, in Hammond, ed., *Letters and Papers,* II, 286; Lafayette to Washington, August 25, 1778, in Sparks, ed., *Letters to Washington,* II, 186; Gottschalk, *Lafayette,* II, 262–63.

18. Sullivan to the President of Congress, August 31, 1778, in Hammond, ed., *Letters and Papers,* II, 180–86; Samuel Ward, Jr., to Phebe Ward, August 27, 1778, Ward MSS, RIHS; "Diary of Major Gibbs," *Pennsylvania Archives,* VI, 735–36; "Journal of Ebenezer Wild," *Proceedings of the Massachusetts Historical Society,* 2nd series, VI, 115–16; Angell, *Diary of Israel Angell,* pp. 7–8; Nathanael Greene to Washington, August 28, 1778, in Greene, *Life of Greene,* II, 126; Green to Washington, August 31, 1778, in Greene, *Life of Greene,* II, 130–32; John Trumbull to Jonathan Trumbull, August 30, 1778, in *Trumbull Papers,* Part IV, 261–63; Map of Military Operations, R.I. State Archives.

130   *The Rhode Island Campaign of 1778*

19. Mackenzie, *Diary*, II, 380–81; Pigot to Clinton, August 31, 1778, in *Rhode Island Historical Tracts*, No. 6, pp. 89–90; von Eelking, "Military Operations," in *Rhode Island Historical Tracts*, No. 6, pp. 55–56; Max von Eelking, *German and Allied Troops in the North American War of Independence*, trans. J. G. Rosengarten (Albany: Joel Munsell's Sons, 1893), p. 166.

20. Mackenzie, *Diary*, II, 381–82; von Eelking, "Military Operations," in *Rhode Island Historical Tracts*, No. 6, p. 56; John Trumbull to Jonathan Trumbull, August 30, 1778, in *Trumbull Papers*, Part IV, 261; Nathanael Greene to Washington, August 31, 1778, in Greene, *Life of Greene*, II, 130.

21. Mackenzie, *Diary*, II, 381; Pigot to Clinton, August 31, 1778, in *Rhode Island Historical Tracts*, No. 6, p. 90.

22. Mackenzie, *Diary*, II, 382; Pigot to Clinton, August 31, 1778, in *Rhode Island Historical Tracts*, No. 6, pp. 90–91; Popp, *Diary of Stephan Popp*, p. 13; von Eelking, "Military Operations," in *Rhode Island Historical Tracts*, No. 6, pp. 58–59; Sullivan to the President of Congress, August 31, 1778, in Hammond, ed., *Letters and Papers*, II, 282–83; Map of Military Operations, R.I. State Archives.

23. The colonel was the son of Connecticut's governor, Jonathan Trumbull, and later became a famous painter. He had served with Washington from Boston to New York, and although he resigned from the Continental Army in April 1777 as a result of a dispute concerning his seniority, he volunteered as deputy adjutant general to Gates during the Saratoga campaign. Boatner, *Encyclopedia of the American Revolution*, pp. 1119–21.

24. Mackenzie, *Diary*, II, 382–83; Pigot to Clinton, August 31, 1778, in *Rhode Island Historical Tracts*, No. 6, pp. 90–91; "Diary of Major Gibbs," *Pennsylvania Archives*, VI, 736; John Trumbull, *Autobiography: Reminiscences and Letters of John Trumbull from 1756 to 1841* (New York, 1841), pp. 53–55; John Trumbull to Jonathan Trumbull, August 30, 1778, in *Trumbull Papers*, Part IV, 261–62; Sullivan to the President of Congress, August 31, 1778, in Hammond, ed., *Letters and Papers*, II, 282–84; Map of Military Operations, R.I. State Archives.

25. Sullivan to the President of Congress, August 31, 1778, in Hammond, ed., *Letters and Papers*, II, 283.

26. Henry J. Cadbury, "A Quaker Travelling in the Wake of War, 1781," *The New England Quarterly*, XXIII (September 1950), 400; Stone, *Allies*, p. 102.

27. Mackenzie, *Diary*, II, 383, 400–02.

28. Mackenzie, *Diary*, II, 383; Sullivan to the President of Congress, August 31, 1778, in Hammond, ed., *Letters and Papers*, II, 283; Samuel Ward, Jr., to Phebe Ward, August 30, 1778, Ward MSS, RIHS; "Diary of Major Gibbs," *Pennsylvania Archives*, VI, 736; "Journal of Ebenezer Wild," *Proceedings of the Massachusetts Historical Society*, 2nd series, VI, 116; von Eelking, "Military Operations," in *Rhode Island Historical Tracts*, No. 6, pp. 60–61; John Trumbull to Jonathan Trumbull, August 30, 1778, in *Trumbull Papers*, Part IV, 262; Peter Colt to Asa Waterman, August 30, 1778, Waterman Papers, RIHS; Map of Military Operations, R.I. State Archives.

29. Lovell's men were the only troops from the second line to go into the actual battle.

30. Sullivan to the President of Congress, August 31, 1778, in Hammond, ed., *Letters and Papers,* II, 283–85; Nathanael Greene to Washington, August 31, 1778, in Greene, *Life of Greene,* II, 130–31; "Diary of Major Gibbs," *Pennsylvania Archives,* VI, 736; "Journal of Ebenezer Wild," *Proceedings of the Massachusetts Historical Society,* 2nd series, VI, 116; von Eelking, "Military Operations," *Rhode Island Historical Tracts,* No. 6, pp. 61–62; Popp, *Diary of Stephan Popp,* p. 13; Angell, *Diary of Israel Angell,* p. 9; Samuel Ward, Jr., to Phebe Ward, August 30, 1778, Ward MSS, RIHS; John Trumbull to Jonathan Trumbull, August 30, 1778, in *Trumbull Papers,* Part IV, 262–63; John Trumbull, *Autobiography,* pp. 54–57; Samuel Smith, *Memoirs of the Life of Samuel Smith: Being an Extract from a Journal Written by Himself from 1776–1786* (Middleborough, Mass., 1853), p. 11; Map of Military Operations, R.I. State Archives.

31. Nathanael Greene to Washington, August 31, 1778, in Greene, *Life of Greene,* II, 131.

32. Sullivan to the President of Congress, August 31, 1778, in Hammond, ed., *Letters and Papers,* II, 284; Angell, *Diary of Israel Angell,* p. 9.

33. Mackenzie, *Diary,* II, 383.

34. Pigot to Clinton, August 31, 1778, in *Rhode Island Historical Tracts,* No. 6, p. 91.

35. Sullivan to the President of Congress, August 31, 1778, in Hammond, ed., *Letters and Papers,* II, 284; "Diary of Major Gibbs," *Pennsylvania Archives,* VI, 736.

36. Peckham, *The Toll of Independence,* p. 54.

37. Pigot to Clinton, August 31, 1778, in *Rhode Island Historical Tracts,* No. 6, p. 93; Lowell, *The Hessians,* pp. 219–20.

38. It should be noted, however, that in comparison with a number of other Revolutionary engagements, the Battle of Rhode Island was hardly among the most sanguine.

39. "Journal of Ebenezer Wild," *Proceedings of the Massachusetts Historical Society,* 2nd series, VI, 116.

40. Sullivan to the President of Congress, August 31, 1778, in Hammond, ed., *Letters and Papers,* II, 285–86; Mackenzie, *Diary,* II, 385–87; Angell, *Diary of Israel Angell,* p. 9; Washington to Sullivan, August 28, 1778, in Fitzpatrick, ed., *Writings of Washington,* XII, 369; "Diary of Major Gibbs," *Pennsylvania Archives,* VI, 736.

41. General Orders and Orderly Book, August 30, 1778, RIHS.

42. Benjamin Quarles, *The Negro in the American Revolution* (Chapel Hill: published for the Institute of Early American History and Culture, Williamsburg, Virginia, by the University of North Carolina Press, 1964), p. 81. In none of his letters of this period contained in the Ward MSS at RIHS is Major Ward critical of the men of his command.

43. Sullivan to the President of Congress, August 31, 1778, in Hammond, ed., *Letters and Papers,* II, 286; Sullivan to Washington, August 31, 1778, in *Ibid.,* p. 287; "Diary of Major Gibbs," *Pennsylvania Archives,* VI, 736; "Journal of Ebenezer Wild," *Proceedings of the Massachusetts Historical Society,* 2nd series, VI, 116–17; Angell, *Diary of Israel Angell,* pp. 10–11; Map of Military Operations, R.I. State Archives. Edwin M. Stone, in *Our French Allies,*

pp. 107–10, provides an interesting and capable discussion of the route of Sullivan's retreat.

44. Mackenzie, *Diary,* II, 387–88.

45. Mackenzie, *Diary,* II, 389–91; Clinton, *American Rebellion,* p. 103.

46. This undertaking was in conformance with Lord Germain's recent instructions to Clinton and was part of a policy designed to pin down for coastal defense the troops that Washington's main army so desperately needed.

47. André, *Major André's Journal,* pp. 87–92, 94–97; Clinton, *American Rebellion,* pp. 103–04; Mackenzie, *Diary,* II, 391.

IX

Diplomacy Triumphs

ALTHOUGH SULLIVAN HAD BEEN COMPELLED to withdraw from Rhode Island and strategically the campaign had ended in defeat, Congress voted its thanks to Sullivan and his army. Proclaiming the action of August 29 to be an American victory, the delegates then defeated a motion by Sullivan's political enemies to reconsider the resolution.[1]

Yet there was also the question of what effect Sullivan's conduct toward d'Estaing and the resentment aroused by the fleet's departure for Boston would have on the new alliance. When he had reached Nantasket Roads and received the protest of Sullivan's officers, the admiral inwardly fumed but maintained his composure.[2] His sole response to the document was to inform Sullivan that it "imposed on the commandant of the King's fleet the grievous but necessary rule of absolute silence."[3] Later, having been informed of Sullivan's perilous position at the northern end of Rhode Island, d'Estaing generously offered to march his troops overland to the Americans' support and place himself under Sullivan's command, stating that

> our honor, demands that the commander should give evidence
> by his conduct and by his sentiments towards Your Excellency
> and by a declaration that the French delicacy cannot have been
> wounded by an impulsive moment followed by mutual regrets.[4]

Clearly d'Estaing was playing the diplomat, for as he later privately expressed his feelings on this occasion, "I offered to become a colonel of infantry, under the command of one who three years ago was a lawyer, and who certainly must have been an uncomfortable man for his clients." [5]

Still other efforts to ease the tense relations that had developed were made by Nathanael Greene. Shortly after Sullivan's protest was drawn up, Greene sought to soothe Lafayette's anger, and, as Lafayette wrote to Washington, "he seems very sensible of what I feel." [6] For a man who believed that the marquis and other French noblemen had been overly attentive to his young and attractive wife during the winter at Valley Forge, and she too receptive, Greene's actions were a model of self-restraint and good sense. [7] Ever reliant on his subordinate's abilities, Washington wrote to Greene stating that "I . . . fully depend upon your exerting yourself to heal all private animosities between our principal Officers and the french, and to prevent all illiberal expressions and reflections that may fall from the Army at large." [8] Thus Greene also sought to apologize to d'Estaing for Sullivan's conduct, eliciting a flattering response from the admiral which assured him that "it is from you and what you are that it is doubtless suitable and flattering to judge of the respectable and amiable qualities of American general officers whom I have not the honor of knowing. . . ." [9] Still later Greene prevailed upon the Rhode Island Assembly not to read aloud Sullivan's censures of the French in a house crowded with spectators. [10]

Washington also took a hand in attempting to allay the ill-will that had sprung up. As early as August 28 he had prudently warned Sullivan:

> Should the expedition fail, thro' the abandonment of the French fleet, the Officers concerned will be apt to complain loudly. But prudence dictates that we should put the best face upon the matter and, to the World, attribute the removal to Boston, to necessity. The Reasons are too obvious to need explaining. [11]

Although it had voted Sullivan its thanks, Congress was
fully cognizant of the strains which Sullivan's actions had
placed upon the alliance. On August 28 it ordered that the
contents of the various documents criticizing d'Estaing be
kept secret, and it enjoined Washington to prevent his officers
from making the dispute a public one. The Congress also
voted to communicate the protests of the army to Gerard, the
French minister at Philadelphia.[12] Gerard, in response, made
it known that he believed that the alliance could not well endure attacks upon the French of the same nature which Sullivan had made.[13] In a secret dispatch to Vergennes, Louis
XVI's Foreign Minister, Gerard noted that "Unfortunately
this is a nation of hot-heads." [14]

On September 1 Washington wrote to the New Hampshire
general once again, instructing him to heed the congressional
directive.[15] The temperamental Sullivan was not so easily si-
lenced, however, for as late as October d'Estaing was writing
to Greene about

> the obstinacy which General Sullivan exhibits in national impu-
> tations; and the abuse of his place in filling incessantly the pub-
> lic papers which are under his direction with things which might
> at length create ill blood between the individuals of two nations
> who are and ought to be united. It is wounding their interests in
> a capital manner to dare by indiscretion or passion to foment
> what ought to be extinguished if it exists. I have been obliged
> lately to entreat General Sullivan to reflect on this subject.[16]

Even while continuing to exacerbate the situation, Sullivan
sought to excuse his conduct by explaining to the admiral
that much of it was caused by enemies who were seeking to
destroy him, a fact that d'Estaing found difficult to appreci-
ate.[17] All the while, Sullivan informed Washington of the
"friendship" that existed between the admiral and himself.[18]

Despite Sullivan's vitriolic pronouncements most American
leaders took a responsible view of the situation, which ac-
corded with national self-interest. From Philadelphia Henry
Marchant, one of Rhode Island's representatives to Congress

and one of its most respected members, wrote to Governor William Greene counseling patience:

> I hope that . . . we may in some good measure suppress observations upon the conduct of others, which may do us no good, but may do harm. Besides, prudence will teach us always to put the most favorable Constructions upon the conduct and opinions of others, and we may sometimes doubt at least whether or no we are not mistaken ourselves. Your Excellency, I presume, will see my meaning. Whether all things considered, it was a right measure in the French fleet going out after the English fleet, and whether the going out the second time was advisable, are points not the most easily to be determined. It is politic, however, that we should be delicate upon the point, if we would not gratify our enemies, the Tories especially. This is certain, that no man could possibly express more uneasiness on that occasion than the French Minister, And whether the Count's conduct was the most prudent or not, the goodness of his intentions cannot be doubted. The friendship of his royal Master most assuredly cannot, and we may depend upon a vigor of conduct that will show his royal resolution to make good his ground, and to anticipate our wishes and expectations in him.[19]

To a friend in Boston where the French fleet lay in port, Samuel Adams, the firebrand of the early days of the Revolution and no great devotee of France, wrote that "in my opinion it would be in a great Degree impolitick at this Juncture to suffer an Odium to be cast on Count d'Estaing. If there should be a disposition to do it I am perswaded Men of Discretion and Influence will check it." [20]

Hancock was particularly active in his efforts to promote good will. Of his work and its effects, Greene wrote Washington that "the Admiral and all the French officers are now upon an exceeding good footing with the gentlemen of the town. General Hancock takes unwearied pains to promote a good understanding. . . . His house is full from morning till night." [21] To this d'Estaing reciprocated by such social pleasantries as inviting Hancock's wife, Dolly, to visit the fleet with her friends, and Mrs. Hancock accepted, bringing five hundred of them.[22] On September 22 d'Estaing and his officers

were received by a delegation composed of members of both
houses of the Massachusetts Assembly. Three days later the
assembly held a state dinner in honor of the Frenchmen.[23]

Yet, for all Hancock's show of good will, there were those
who were unconvinced by his display. James Warren,
Hancock's inveterate political enemy, attributed it largely to
Hancock's desire to win the president's office in Massachusetts, and wrote to Samuel Adams: "he is making great Enter-
tainments and figureing away in a most Magnificent manner.
The Eyes of many People are open and see his views and Motives." [24] In addition, Abigail Adams felt constrained to inform her husband John that for all the efforts of Hancock and
General Heath to spread good will, "very few if any private
families have any acquaintance with" the French, and that
they had been "neglected" by the town.[25]

Despite all of the courtesy that was displayed among the
higher circles of Allied leadership, conditions below the surface remained ugly. With the fleet's arrival prices in Boston
were immediately raised by the town's enterprising mer-
chants, an act which the French did not fail to note. At the
same time, the increased cost of living aroused further resentment toward the French on the part of the native population.[26]

Even while Hancock, Greene, and General Heath attempted to lessen tensions, another galling incident took
place. On September 8 a mob attacked a bakery in Boston
which d'Estaing had established to supply his fleet. In the
affray two French officers were wounded. Six days later one of
them, the Chevalier de St. Sauveur, died. Greene reported to
Washington that the incident had been inspired by troops belonging to the Convention Army of Burgoyne, then being held
prisoners at Boston, and British seamen serving aboard
American privateers. This constituted the official American
explanation of the affair, and outwardly the French seemed to
accept it.[27] St. Sauveur's remains were quietly buried by candlelight in the "Stranger's Tomb" beneath King's Chapel. In a

conciliatory gesture the Massachusetts Assembly voted to erect a cenotaph to the young officer's memory. This cenotaph, however, was not constructed until 1917, when America was showing her fervor for her new ally in the war against Germany.

Concealing whatever bitterness he may have felt, d'Estaing wrote to Washington, "we accused fate only." [28] Still other riots occurred on September 26 and 27 and on October 5.[29] For all of this, little blame was attached to the French themselves. As James Warren wrote, "the French officers and Seamen in this Squadron behave themselves Extreemly well; they are indeed the most peaceable, quiet and orderly set of men in their profession I ever saw. . . ." [30]

Certainly American attitudes toward France had not been improved by the events of August. Writing to his father, John Laurens observed, "I saw very plainly when I was at Boston, that our ancient hereditary prejudices were very far from being eradicated." [31] Yet if France was not loved, American statesmen realized that she was useful. On October 17 Congress passed a resolution formally thanking d'Estaing for his aid, and declaring that "his Excellency, and the officers and men under his command, have rendered every benefit to these states, which circumstances and nature of the service would admit of, and are fully entitled to the regards of the friends of America." [32] Five days later Congress drew up the following instructions to Franklin in Paris:

> You are immediately to assure his most Christian Majesty, that these states entertain the highest sense of his exertions in their favour, particularly by sending the respectable squadron under the Count d'Estaing, which would probably have terminated the war in a speedy and honourable manner, if unforseen and unfortunate circumstances had not intervened.
>
> You are further to assure him that they consider this speedy aid, not only as a testimony of his Majesty's fidelity to the engagements he hath entered into, but as an earnest of that protection which they hope from his power and magnanimity, and as a bond of gratitude to the union, founded on mutual interest.[33]

Finally, in November of 1778, with the completion of the repairs which his ships required, d'Estaing and his fleet sailed from Boston for operations in the Caribbean. In the autumn of 1779 the French admiral was to return to the American coast, where he was to suffer a terrible defeat at Savannah while acting in conjunction with General Benjamin Lincoln, a far more diplomatic man than Sullivan. Although it did not result in the bitterness of the Newport experience, the defeat continued the general American sense of disappointment with the alliance.[34] It was this feeling of unrealized hopes, and even resentment, to which Rochambeau fell heir in 1780, and which he was skillful enough to overcome.[35]

What prevented the Newport crisis from becoming fatal to the Franco-American alliance was a rational assessment by both sides of their mutual interests. American leaders, both military and political, were not influenced by sentimental considerations of French courtliness or personal gallantry. Instead, their decisions were made upon the basis of a realistic recognition of how vital French financial, diplomatic, and military aid was to the success of the American war effort, a fact which became increasingly evident as the War for Independence dragged on in the years following the Rhode Island campaign.[36]

Notes

1. Ford, ed., *Journals of the Continental Congress,* XII, 894–95.

2. Lafayette to Washington, September 1, 1778, in Sparks, ed., *Letters to Washington,* II, 198–99.

3. D'Estaing to Sullivan, August 30, 1778, in Hammond, ed., *Letters and Papers,* II, 277.

4. D'Estaing to Sullivan, August 30, 1778, in Hammond, ed., *Letters and Papers,* II, 278–79.

5. D'Estaing to the Minister of Marine, November 5, 1778, in Doniol, *Histoire,* III, 363.

6. Lafayette to Washington, August 25, 1778, in Sparks, ed., *Letters to Washington,* II, 188.

7. Thayer, *Nathanael Greene,* pp. 223–24.

8. Washington to Greene, September 1, 1778, in Fitzpatrick, ed., *Writings of Washington,* XII, 387.

9. D'Estaing to Greene, October 1, 1778, in Greene, *Life of Greene,* II, 148.

10. Greene, *Life of Greene,* II, 149–50.

11. Washington to Sullivan, August 28, 1778, in Fitzpatrick, ed., *Writings of Washington,* XII, 369.

12. Ford, *Journal of the Continental Congress,* XII, 848–49.

13. Henry Laurens to Washington, August 29, 1778, in Burnett, ed., *Letters of Members of the Continental Congress,* III, 392–93; William C. Stinchcombe, *The American Revolution and the French Alliance* (Syracuse: Syracuse University Press, 1969), p. 55.

14. Stone, *Allies,* p. 78.

15. Washington to Sullivan, September 1, 1778, in Fitzpatrick, ed., *Writings of Washington,* XII, 385–86.

16. D'Estaing to Greene, October 1, 1778, in Greene, *Life of Greene,* II, 149.

17. D'Estaing to Greene, October 1, 1778, in Greene, *Life of Greene,* II, 148.

18. Sullivan to Washington, September 3, 1778, in Hammond, ed., *Letters and Papers,* II, 300.

19. Henry Marchant to Governor Greene, September 6, 1778, in Staples, *Rhode Island in the Continental Congress,* p. 199.

20. Samuel Adams to James Warren, September 12, 1778, in Burnett, ed., *Letters of Members of the Continental Congress,* III, 409. Adams also wrote a similar letter to Samuel Savage on September 14, 1778; see *Ibid.,* p. 410.

21. Nathanael Greene to Washington, September 16, 1778, in Greene, *Life of Greene,* II, 143–44.

22. H. S. Allan, *John Hancock: Patriot in Purple* (New York: Macmillan Co., 1948), p. 289.

23. Heath, *Memoirs,* pp. 206–07.

24. James Warren to Adams, October 7, 1778, in *Warren-Adams Letters, Being Chiefly a Correspondence among John Adams, Samuel Adams, and James Warren, Massachusetts Historical Society Collections,* LXXIII, 2 vols. (Boston: Massachusetts Historical Society, 1917), II, 52–53.

25. Abigail Adams to John Adams, October 25, 1778, in Lyman H. Butterfield and Marc Friedlaender, eds., *Adams Family Correspondence* (Cambridge: Harvard University Press, 1973), III, 110.

26. *Extrait de journal,* pp. 29–31; William Stewart to William Goddard, September 10, 1778, Military Papers, V, 35, RIHS. It should be noted that the inflated prices which the French paid for flour and provisions for the fleet totally disrupted the procurement efforts of the commissary of purchases in both Massachusetts and upstate New York. Chester M. Destler, *Connecticut: The Provisions State* (Chester, Conn.: Pequot Press, 1973), p. 35.

27. Heath to the Council of Massachusetts, September 9, 1778, in *Heath Papers,* Part II, 267; Heath to Washington, in *Ibid.,* pp. 271–72; Heath, *Memoirs,* p. 206; Nathanael Greene to Washington, September 16, 1778, in Greene, *Life of Greene,* II, 143; Washington to d'Estaing, September 29, 1778, in Fitzpatrick, ed., *Writings of Washington,* XII, 516–17; John Laurens to Henry Laurens, September 24, 1778, in Laurens, *Army Correspondence,* pp. 227–28; *Extrait de journal,* p. 28.

28. D'Estaing to Washington, September 25, 1778, in *Washington, sa Correspondance,* p. 14.

29. Stinchcombe, *The French Alliance*, p. 59.

30. James Warren to John Adams, October 7, 1778, in *Warren-Adams Letters*, II, 51.

31. John Laurens to Henry Laurens, September 24, 1778, in Laurens, *Army Correspondence*, p. 228.

32. Ford, ed., *Journals of the Continental Congress*, XXII, 1021.

33. *Secret Journals of the Acts and Proceedings of Congress, from the First Meeting Thereof to the Dissolution of the Confederation, by the Adoption of the Constitution of the United States*, 4 vols. (Boston: Thomas B. Wait, 1821), II, 108.

34. Stinchcombe, *The French Alliance*, p. 78.

35. *Ibid.*, pp. 135–36; Arnold Whitridge, *Rochambeau* (New York: Macmillan Co., 1965), p. 87. For contemporary accounts describing the reaction to Rochambeau's arrival in America and how he dealt with it, see Louis Jean Baptiste Silvestre de Robernier, "Journal of the War in America, 1780–1783," a typescript translation of the original in the RIHS; Robin, *New Travels through North-America* (Philadelphia: Robert Bell, 1783), and Yeager, "The French Fleet at Newport, 1780–1781," *Rhode Island History*, XXX (Summer 1971); Howard C. Rice, Jr., and Anne S. K. Brown, *The American Campaigns of Rochambeau's Army*, 2 vols., Vol. I: *The Journals* (Princeton: Princeton University Press, 1972).

36. Stinchcombe, *The French Alliance*, pp. 48–61, 200–13. Stinchcombe's book is far and away the best diplomatic study of the Rhode Island crisis. However, as it focuses on an analysis of American public opinion, it is somewhat lacking in terms of how deeply the events which transpired from August through October 1778 affected the French government in Paris.

Epilogue

WITH THE RHODE ISLAND campaign over, Sullivan soon found himself in the same position that he had occupied before d'Estaing arrived. By September 4 his army had virtually disappeared, leaving him with only twelve hundred Continentals and two thousand state troops and militia, most of whose time was to expire in a few days. Thus he was once more forced to plead with Rhode Island's neighboring states for men to defend his department, and this time he went largely unheard.[1]

Yet d'Estaing's presence in North American waters had not been completely without effect. Although the Allies failed to take either New York or Newport, the French fleet's arrival had prevented Clinton and Howe from taking offensive action for two months, and it delayed Clinton's dispatch of an expedition to France's vital possessions in the West Indies until November. The experience at Rhode Island had also been psychologically damaging to the British, and when d'Estaing sailed for the northern Atlantic again in 1779, Clinton feared a repetition of the siege at Newport and abandoned Rhode Island in October of that year. Thus the port was left open for Ternay and Rochambeau when they arrived in 1780.[2]

As for the principal actors in the drama of the summer of 1778, Sullivan left Rhode Island in March of 1779 to conduct a moderately successful campaign against the Six Nations in New York's Finger Lakes area. Seeking a temporary leave to recover his health in November of 1779, he submitted his resignation from the army in the expectation that Congress would be coerced into letting him return home for a time. To his surprise and indignation it accepted the resignation instead. Turning to politics, he became governor of his state and enjoyed a good deal of success in the political sphere. Alcohol, however, got the best of him; he drank himself to death, succumbing to its ravages and the effects of rapid senility on January 23, 1795.[3]

When d'Estaing returned to France he was instrumental in influencing his government to send Rochambeau's army to America. During the French Revolution the admiral joined the moderate reform faction, but for his involvement in an attempt to rescue Marie Antoinette and for alleged bribe taking, he went to his death on the guillotine on April 28, 1794.[4]

Following his successful defense of Newport, Sir Robert Pigot left Rhode Island for England in September 1778. He was to share none of the stigma which attended the eventual defeat of Britain in the American struggle. The years that remained to him were quiescent ones, as suited a baronet, a title to which he had succeeded in 1777.[5]

After the war Newport never returned to its commercial greatness, and for years it lacked its antebellum splendor. During the siege of 1778 Paul Revere had written to his wife:

> you have heard this Island is the Garden of America, indeed it used to appear so; but those British Savages have so abused & destroyed the Trees (the greatest part of which was Fruit Trees), that it does not look like the same Island; some of the Inhabitants who left it hardly know where to find their homes.[6]

In monetary value alone Newport reported $412,920 worth of damages, while Middletown fixed its losses at better than $130,000. The island had lost much of its population, and as a trading center it was soon permanently overshadowed by

Providence. Such was the legacy of war and an often forgotten campaign.[7]

Notes

1. Sullivan to the Massachusetts Council, September 4, 1778, in Hammond, ed., *Letters and Papers,* II, 301.

2. Willcox, *Portrait of a General,* pp. 257–58, 291–92; Alden, *A History of the American Revolution,* pp. 396–98; Wallace, *Appeal to Arms,* pp. 194–95.

3. Whittemore, *A General of the Revolution, passim.*

4. Boatner, *Encyclopedia of the American Revolution,* p. 350.

5. Boatner, *Encyclopedia of the American Revolution,* p. 868.

6. "Letter of Paul Revere," in *Massachusetts Historical Society Proceedings,* XIII, 251.

7. Polishook, *Rhode Island and the Union,* pp. 46–47. See also Patrick T. Conley, "Revolution's Impact on Rhode Island," *Rhode Island History,* XXXIV (November 1975), 121–28; and Nancy Fisher Chudacoff, "The Revolution and the Town: Providence 1775–1783," *Rhode Island History,* XXXV (August 1976), 71–89.

Select Bibliography

PRIMARY MATERIALS

I. MANUSCRIPTS

A. *Newport Historical Society*
   Henry Sherburne Military Book, 1778.
   Miscellaneous MSS.
B. *Redwood Library*
   Order Book of the American Forces in the Battle of Rhode Island.
C. *Rhode Island Historical Society*
   Book of Depositions, 1776–1793. Ships' Protests Showing Loss of
      Vessels and Enemy Action during the Revolution; Bonds; En-
      listments in the Army; Promises to Pay; List of Newport, R.I.,
      Town Records, 1778.
   Book of General Orders Belonging to the Adjutant of Colonel
      Greene's Regiment, 1778. Ward Papers.
   Captain Stephen Olney's account of that part of the Revolutionary
      War in which he took part. Olney Papers.
   Diary of Reverend Enos Hitchcock, 1778.
   Diary of Reverend John Pitman, 1777–1781.
   General Orders and Orderly Book of a Part of the Army under Gen-
      eral Sullivan, 1st June–August 25th, 1778.
   Hitchcock Papers.
   Military Papers. Vol. V.
   Miscellaneous MSS. Bowen Papers: Letters to William Bowen
      . . . from Stephen Olney, 1764–1794.
   Nathanael Greene Papers.
   Noah Robinson. Journal of a Six Months' Campaign.
   Olney Papers. Jeremiah Olney. 1755–1820. 3 vols.

Orderly Book of a Division of the Rhode Island Troops under the Immediate Command of General James M. Varnum, Which Formed a Portion of the Continental Army under General John Sullivan during the Operations in Rhode Island from May 20, 1778 to February 12, 1779.

Orderly Book of Colonel Christopher Greene. 2 vols.

Papers of Asa Waterman, Rhode Island Revolutionary War Deputy Commissioner, 1775–1781.

Peck MSS Collection.

Personal Papers of Captain Oliver Spink, a Rhode Island Revolutionary Soldier, 1747–1843.

Rhode Island Historical Society MSS.

Updike Papers.

Ward MSS, 1762–1778.

D. *Rhode Island State Archives*

Journals of the Council of War in Rhode Island. 4 vols.

Letters from the Governors of Rhode Island, 1775–1778.

Letters to the Governors of Rhode Island, 1775–1778.

Papers of Asa Waterman, Rhode Island Revolutionary War Deputy Commissioner, 1775–1781.

Petitions to the Rhode Island General Assembly, 1775–1778.

II. PRINTED MATERIALS (Diaries, letters, military records, etc.)

Almy, Mary. "Mrs. Almy's Journal." *Newport Historical Magazine,* I (July 1880), 17–36.

André, John. *Major André's Journal: Operations of the British Army under Lieutenant Generals Sir William Howe and Sir Henry Clinton, June 1777 to November 1778.* Tarrytown: William Abbott, 1930.

Angell, Israel, *The Diary of Israel Angell.* Ed. Edward Field. Providence: Preston & Rounds Co., 1899.

Balderston, Marion, and Syrett, David, eds. *The Lost War: Letters from British Officers during the American Revolution.* New York: Horizon Press, 1975.

Bartlett, John R., ed. *The Records of the Colony of Rhode Island and Providence Plantations in New England.* 10 vols. Providence: A. C. Greene & Bros., 1856–65.

Baurmeister, Carl Leopold. *Revolution in America: Confidential Letters and Journals, 1776–1784, of Adjutant General Major Baurmeister of the Hessian Forces.* Trans. and annotated by Bernhard A. Uhlendorf. New Brunswick, N.J.: Rutgers University Press, 1957.

Burnett, Edmund Cody, ed. *Letters of Members of the Continental Congress.* 8 vols. Washington, D.C.: Carnegie Institution of Washington, 1921–38.

Butterfield, Lyman H., and Friedlaender, Marc, eds. *Adams Family Correspondence.* Vol. III: April 1778–September 1780. Cambridge: Harvard University Press, 1973.

"Centennial Celebration of the Battle of Rhode Island, at Portsmouth, R.I., August 29, 1878. Comprising the Oration by Ex-United States Senator Samuel G. Arnold; A letter of Sir Henry Pigot, the English Commander; A German Account of the Battle; The Views of General Lafayette." *Rhode Island Historical Tracts,* No. 6. Providence: Sidney S. Rider, 1878.

Clark, William Bell, ed. *Naval Documents of the American Revolution.* 7 vols. to date. Washington, D.C.: Government Printing Office, 1964–.

Clinton, Sir Henry. *The American Rebellion: Sir Henry Clinton's Narrative of His Campaigns, 1775–82.* Ed. William B. Willcox. New Haven: Yale University Press, 1954.

Commager, Henry Steele, and Morris, Richard B., eds. *The Spirit of "Seventy-Six: The Story of the American Revolution as Told by Participants.* 2 vols. New York: Harper & Row, 1958.

"Conduct of the Black Regiment in the Action of August 29th, 1778, on Rhode Island, as Given by the Orderly Books of the Army." *Rhode Island Historical Tracts,* No. 6. Providence: Sidney S. Rider, 1878.

Connecticut Military Record: Records of Connecticut Men in the War of the Revolution. Compiled by authority of the General Assembly under direction of the Adjutants-General. Hartford, 1889.

Cunningham, Anne Rowe, ed. *Letters and Diary of John Rowe, Boston Merchant, 1759–1762, 1764–1779.* Boston: W. B. Clarke Co., 1903.

Cutler, William Parker, and Perkins, Julia. *Life, Journals and Correspondence of Reverend Manasseh Cutler.* 2 vols. Cincinnati: Robert Clarke & Co., 1888.

Doniol, Henri. *Histoire de la Participation de la France à l'establishment des Etats-Unis d'Amérique.* 6 vols. Paris, 1884–92.

Estaing, C. H. T., Comte d'. *Declaration adressée au Nom du Roi a tous les anciens François de l'Amérique Septentrionale. A Bord du Languedoc.* John Carter Brown Library, Providence, R.I.

————, and Washington, George. *Washington, sa Correspondance avec d'Estaing.* Paris: Publié par les Soins de la Fondation Nationale pour la Reproduction des Manuscripts Précieux et Pièces Rares d'Archives, 1937.

Extrait de journal d'un officier marine avec le Comte d'Estaing dans les Etats-Unis. N.p., n.d.

Farnsworth, Amos. "Amos Farnsworth's Diary." *Massachusetts Historical Society Proceedings,* 2nd series, XII (1897–99), 78–102.

Fitzpatrick, J. C., ed. *The Writings of George Washington.* 39 vols. Washington, D.C.: Government Printing Office, 1931–44.

Ford, Worthington C., ed. *Journals of the Continental Congress.* 34 vols. Washington, D.C.: Government Printing Office, 1904–37.

Fortescue, John W., ed. *The Correspondence of King George III.* 6 vols. London, 1927–28.

Gardiner, C. Harvey, ed. *A Study in Dissent: The Warren-Gerry Correspondence, 1776–1792.* Carbondale and Edwardsville: Southern Illinois University Press, 1968.

Graydon, Alexander. *Memoirs of His Own Time with Reminiscences of the Men and Events of the Revolution.* Ed. John Stockton Littell. Philadelphia: Lindsay & Blakiston, 1846.

Greene, Fleet S. "Newport in the Hands of the British: A Diary of the Revolution." *The Historical Magazine,* IV (1860), serialized.

Greene, George W. *The Life of Nathanael Greene, Major-General in the Army of the Revolution.* 3 vols. New York: Hurd & Houghton, 1867–71.

Hammond, O. G., ed. *Letters and Papers of Major General John Sullivan. Collections of the New Hampshire Historical Society,* XIII–XV. 3 vols. Concord, N.H.: New Hampshire Historical Society, 1930–39.

The Heath Papers. Parts II, III. *Massachusetts Historical Society Collections,* 7th series, IV, V. Boston: Massachusetts Historical Society, 1904–05.

Heath, William. *Heath's Memoirs of the American War.* Ed. R. R. Wilson. New York, 1904.

Howland, John. *Notices of the Military Services Rendered by the Militia, as Well as by the Enlisted Troops, of the State of Rhode Island, During the Revolutionary War.* Providence, 1832.

Jones, Matt B. "Revolutionary Correspondence of Governor Nicholas Cooke, 1775–1781." *Proceedings of the American Antiquarian Society, New Series, XXXVI,* Part 2 (October 20, 1926), 231–353.

Knollenberg, Bernhard, ed. *Correspondence of Governor Samuel Ward, May 1775–March 1776.* Providence: Rhode Island Historical Society, 1952.

Lafayette, Marquis de. *Letters . . . to Washington, 1777–1779.* Ed. Louis Gottschalk. New York: privately printed by Helen F. Hubbard, 1944.

Laurens, John. *The Army Correspondence of Colonel John Laurens in the Years 1777–1778: Now First Printed from Original Letters to His Father, Henry Laurens, President of the Congress, with a Memoir by William Gilmore Simms.* New York: Bradford Club, 1867.

Lesser, Charles H., ed. *The Sinews of Independence: Monthly Strength Reports of the Continental Army.* Chicago: University of Chicago Press, 1976.

Mackenzie, Frederick. *The Diary of Frederick Mackenzie, Giving a Daily Narrative of His Military Service as an Officer of the Regiment of Royal Welsh Fusiliers during the Years 1775–1781 in Massachusetts, Rhode Island, and New York.* 2 vols. Cambridge: Harvard University Press, 1930.

Moore, Frank, comp. *Diary of the American Revolution.* 2 vols. New York: C. Scribner, 1860.

Moré, Charles A. *The Chevalier de Pontgibaud, a French Volunteer.* Trans. and ed. Robert B. Douglas. Paris: Charles Carrington, 1898.

"Notes on Rhode Island in the Revolution." *Rhode Island Historical Society Proceedings,* 1877–78, pp. 83–101.

O'Beirne, Thomas L. *A Candid and Impartial Narrative of the Transac-*

tions of the Fleet, under the Command of Lord Howe from the Arrival of the Toulon Squadron, on the Coast of America, to the Time of His Lordship's Departure for England. 2nd ed. London: printed for J. Almon, n.d.

"Orders of the Council of War, 1778." *Rhode Island Historical Society Proceedings,* 1878–79, pp. 63–76.

"Original Letters and Documents." *Pennsylvania Magazine of History and Biography,* V (1881), 470–77.

"Part of a Diary of Major Gibbs, 1778." *Pennsylvania Archives,* VI (1853), 734–36.

Peckham, Howard H., ed. *The Toll of Independence: Engagements and Battle Casualties of the American Revolution.* Chicago: University of Chicago Press, 1974.

Popp, Stephan. *A Hessian Soldier in the American Revolution: The Diary of Stephan Popp.* Trans. Reinhart J. Pope. N.p.: privately printed, 1953.

Rankin, Hugh F., and Scheer, George F. *Rebels and Redcoats.* New York: World Publishing Co., 1957.

Revere, Paul. "Letter of Paul Revere." *Massachusetts Historical Society Proceedings,* XIII (February 1874), 251–52.

"Revolutionary Correspondence from 1775 to 1782." *Rhode Island Historical Society Collections,* VI (1867), 107–304, 371–77.

Rhode Island Historical Society. Broadside File.

Rhode Island Historical Society Collections, XXV (1932), 115.

Rhode Island Historical Society. Journal of the War in America, 1780–1783, by Louis Jean Baptiste Silvestre de Robernier, Lieutenant of the Soissonais Regiment in the Army of Rochambeau. Trans. Professor Edouard R. Massey. [Typescript.]

Rice, Howard C., Jr., and Brown, Anne S. K., eds. *The American Campaigns of Rochambeau's Army, 1780–1783.* 2 vols. Princeton: Princeton University Press, 1972.

Robin. *New Travels through North-America: In a Series of Letters Exhibiting the History of the Victorious Campaign of the Allied Armies under His Excellency General Washington and the Count de Rochambeau in the Year 1781.* Translated from the original of the Abbé Robin, one of the chaplains to the French army in America. Philadelphia: Robert Bell, 1783.

Secret Journals of the Acts and Proceedings of Congress, from the First Meeting Thereof to the Dissolution of the Confederation, by the Adoption of the Constitution of the United States. 4 vols. Boston: Thomas B. Wait, 1821.

Showman, Richard K., ed. *The Papers of General Nathanael Greene.* 2 vols. to date. Chapel Hill: University of North Carolina Press for the Rhode Island Historical Society, 1976–.

Smith, Samuel. *Memoirs of the Life of Samuel Smith: Being an Extract from a Journal Written by Himself from 1776–1786.* Middleborough, Mass., 1853.

Sparks, Jared, ed. *Correspondence of the American Revolution: Being*

Letters of Eminent Men to George Washington. 3 vols. Boston: Little, Brown & Co., 1853.

Staples, William R. *Rhode Island in the Continental Congress.* Providence: Providence Press Co., 1870.

Stevens, B. F., ed. *Facsimiles of Manuscripts in European Archives Relating to America, 1773–1783.* 25 vols. London: Whittingham & Co., 1898.

Stiles, Ezra. *The Literary Diary of Ezra Stiles.* Ed. Franklin Bowditch Dexter. 3 vols. New York: Charles Scribner's Sons, 1901.

Stone, Edwin M. *The Life and Recollections of John Howland.* Providence: George H. Whitney, 1857.

Stone, William L., ed. *Letters of Brunswick and Hessian Officers during the American Revolution.* Albany: Joel Munsell's Sons, 1891.

———, ed. *Letters of German Soldiers in the American Revolution.* Albany: Joel Munsell's Sons, 1891.

Trumbull, John T. *Autobiography: Reminiscences and Letters of John Trumbull from 1756–1841.* New York, 1841.

The Trumbull Papers. Part IV. *Massachusetts Historical Society Collections,* 7th series, III. Boston: Massachusetts Historical Society, 1902.

Upham, William P. "A Memoir of General John Glover of Marblehead." *Historical Collections of the Essex Institute,* V (1863), serialized.

von Eelking, Max. *German Allied Troops in the North American War of Independence.* Trans. J. G. Rosengarten. Albany: Joel Munsell's Sons, 1893.

Warren-Adams Letters, Being Chiefly a Correspondence among John Adams, Samuel Adams, and James Warren. 2 vols. *Massachusetts Historical Society Collections,* LXXII, LXXIII. Boston: Massachusetts Historical Society, 1917, 1925.

Watson, W. C. *Men and Times of the Revolution; Or, Memoirs of Elkanah Watson.* 2nd ed. N.p., 1856.

Wild, Ebenezer. "Journal of Ebenezer Wild." *Proceedings of the Massachusetts Historical Society,* 2nd series, VI (October 1890), 78–117.

Yeager, Henry J. "The French Fleet at Newport, 1780–1781." *Rhode Island History,* XXX (August 1971), 86–93.

III. NEWSPAPERS

The Newport Gazette. 1777–1778.

The Newport Mercury. 1775–1776.

The Providence Gazette. 1775–1778.

Rhode Island Historical Society. Revolutionary Newspaper Items Relating to Rhode Island. Typewritten.

IV. MAPS

British Museum. *A Plan of Rhode Island with its Harbour & adjacent Parts shewing the situation of the British Ships & Forces when the French Fleet anchored off the Harbour July 29th, 1778.*

Polk's Rhode Island & Southern Massachusetts Street Map Atlas. Boston: R. L. Polk & Co., 1968.

Rhode Island State Archives. *Map of Military Operations on Rhode Island, 1778.*

SECONDARY MATERIALS

I. BOOKS

Alden, John Richard. *The American Revolution, 1775–1783.* Vol. XI of The New American Nation Series. Ed. H. S. Commager and R. B. Morris. 47 vols. New York: Harper & Row, 1954.

———. *A History of the American Revolution.* New York: Alfred A. Knopf, 1969.

Allan, H. S. *John Hancock: Patriot in Purple.* New York: Macmillan Co., 1948.

Allan, G. W. *A Naval History of the American Revolution.* 2 vols. Boston: Houghton Mifflin Co., 1913.

Allen, Zachariah. *Memorial of Lafayette.* Providence: Bradford, Miller & Simons, n.d.

Amory, Thomas C. *Centennial Memoir of Major-General John Sullivan.* Philadelphia: Collins, 1879.

———. *General John Sullivan: A Vindication of His Character as a Soldier and a Patriot.* Morrisania, N.Y., 1867.

———. *General Sullivan Not a Pensioner of Luzerne.* Boston, 1875.

———. *The Military Services and Public Life of Major-General John Sullivan of the American Revolutionary Army.* Albany: Joel Munsell, 1868.

Anderson, Troyer S. *The Command of the Howe Brothers during the American Revolution.* New York: Oxford University Press, 1936.

Arnold, Samuel Greene. *A History of Rhode Island.* 2 vols. New York: D. Appleton & Co., 1860.

Baker, Virginia. *The History of Warren, Rhode Island, in the War of the Revolution, 1776–1783.* Warren, 1901.

Balch, Thomas W. *The French in America during the War of Independence.* 2 vols. Philadelphia, 1891.

Bancroft, George. *History of the United States, From the Discovery of the Continent.* 10 vols. Boston: Little, Brown & Co., 1834–74.

Battle, Charles A. *Negroes on the Island of Rhode Island.* Newport, 1932.

Bemis, Samuel Flagg. *The Diplomacy of the American Revolution.* New York, 1935.

Berg, Fred Anderson. *Encyclopedia of Continental Army Units: Battalions, Regiments and Independent Corps.* Harrisburg, Pa.: Stackpole Books, 1972.

Billias, George Athan. *General John Glover and His Marblehead Mariners.* New York: Holt, Rinehart & Winston, 1960.

———. ed. *George Washington's Generals.* New York: William Morrow & Co., 1964.

————. *George Washington's Opponents: British Generals and Admirals in the American Revolution.* New York: William Morrow & Co., 1969.

Boatner, Mark M. *Encyclopedia of the American Revolution.* New York: David McKay Co., Inc., 1966.

————. *Landmarks of the American Revolution.* Harrisburg, Pa.: Stackpole Books, 1973.

Bonsal, Stephen. *When the French Were Here.* New York, 1945.

Bridenbaugh, Carl. *Cities in Revolt: Urban Life in America, 1743–1776.* New York, 1955.

Brown, Wallace K. *The Good Americans: The Loyalists in the American Revolution.* New York: William Morrow & Co., 1969.

————. *The King's Friends: The Composition and Motives of the American Loyalist Claimants.* Providence: Brown University Press, 1966.

Burges, Tristam. *The Plough and the Sickle; or Rhode Island in the War of the Revolution of 1776.* Providence, 1846.

Burnett, Edward C. *The Continental Congress.* New York: Macmillan Co., 1942.

Carrington, Henry B. *Battles of the American Revolution.* New York: A. S. Barnes, 1888.

Conley, Patrick T., and Smith, Matthew J. *Catholicism in Rhode Island: The Formative Era.* Diocese of Providence, 1976.

Corwin, Edwin S. *French Policy and the American Alliance of 1778.* Princeton: Princeton University Press, 1916.

Cowell, Benjamin. *The Spirit of '76 in Rhode Island.* Boston: A. J. Wright, 1850.

Cullum, George W. *Historical Sketch of the Fortification Defenses of Narragansett Bay.* Washington, D.C.: 1884.

Destler, Chester M. *Connecticut: The Provisions State.* Chester, Conn.: Pequot Press, 1973.

Diman, J. Lewis. "The Capture of General Richard Prescott by Lt. Col. William Barton." *Rhode Island Historical Tracts,* No. 1. Providence: Sidney S. Rider, 1877.

Dull, Jonathan R. *The French Navy and American Independence: A Study of Arms and Diplomacy, 1774–1787.* Princeton: Princeton University Press, 1975.

Dupuy, R. Ernest and Trevor N. *The Compact History of the Revolutionary War.* New York: Hawthorne Books, Inc., 1963.

Federal Writers' Project of the Works Progress Administration for the State of Rhode Island. *Rhode Island: A Guide to the Smallest State.* Boston: Houghton Mifflin Co., 1937.

Field, Edward. *Revolutionary Defences in Rhode Island.* Providence: Preston and Rounds, 1896.

————, ed. *The State of Rhode Island and Providence Plantations at the End of the Century: A History.* 3 vols. Boston & Syracuse: Mason Publishing Co., 1902.

Flexner, James Thomas. *The Benedict Arnold Case.* New York: Crowell-Collier Publishing Co., 1962.

——— . *George Washington*. Vol. II: *George Washington in the American Revolution, 1775–1783*. Boston: Little, Brown & Co., 1967.

——— . *The Young Hamilton: A Biography*. Boston: Little, Brown & Co., 1978.

Forbes, Allen. *France and New England*. 3 vols. Boston: printed for the State Street Trust Company of Boston by Walton Advertising & Printing Co., 1927.

Forbes, Esther, *Paul Revere and the World He Lived In*. Boston: Houghton Mifflin Co., 1942.

Fortescue, J. W. *A History of the British Army*. 13 vols. in 20. New York: Macmillan Co., 1889–1930.

Freeman, Douglas Southall. *George Washington*. 7 vols. New York: Charles Scribner's Sons, 1948–57.

Gardiner, Asa Bird. *The Battle of Rhode Island*. Providence: Society of the Cincinnati, 1911.

——— . *The Rhode Island Line in the Continental Army and Its Society of the Cincinnati*. Providence: Providence Press Co., 1878.

Goss, E. H. *The Life of Colonel Paul Revere*. 2 vols. Boston: J. G. Cupples Co., 1891.

Gottschalk, Louis. *Lafayette*. Vol. II: *Lafayette Joins the American Army*. Chicago: University of Chicago Press, 1937.

Greene, Francis V. *General Greene*. New York: D. Appleton & Co., 1893.

——— . *The Revolutionary War and the Military Policy of the United States*. New York: D. Appleton & Co., 1911.

Gruber, Ira D. *The Howe Brothers and the American Revolution*. Chapel Hill: University of North Carolina Press, 1972.

Hedges, James B. *The Browns of Providence Plantations, Colonial Years*. Cambridge, Mass.: Harvard University Press, 1952.

James, Sidney V. *Colonial Rhode Island: A History*. New York: Charles Scribner's Sons, 1975.

James, William M. *The British Navy in Adversity*. New York: Longmans, Greene & Co., 1926.

Jones, Thomas. *History of New York during the Revolutionary War*. Ed. Floyd DeLancey. 2 vols. New York: New York Historical Society, 1879.

Jordan, Winthrop D. *White Over Black: American Attitudes Toward the Negro, 1550–1812*. Chapel Hill: published for the Institute of Early American History and Culture by the University of North Carolina Press, 1968.

Ketchum, Richard M., ed. *The American Heritage Book of the Revolution*. New York: American Heritage Publishing Co., Inc., Book Trade Distribution by Simon & Schuster, Inc., 1958.

Knox, Dudley W. *The Naval Genius of George Washington*. Boston: Houghton Mifflin Co., 1932.

Lawrence, Alexander A. *Storm Over Savannah: The Story of Count d'Estaing and the Siege of the Town in 1779*. Athens: University of Georgia Press, 1951.

Lewis, Charles Lee. *Admiral de Grasse and American Independence.* Annapolis: U.S. Naval Institute, 1945.

The Life and Surprising Adventures of Captain Silas Talbot. London: printed by Barnard and Sultzer for Tegg and Castleman, 1803.

Livermore, George. *An Historical Research Respecting the Opinions of the Founders of the Republic on Negroes as Slaves, as Citizens, and as Soldiers.* Boston, 1863.

Lossing, Benson. *Pictorial Field Book of the American Revolution.* 2 vols. New York, 1851.

Lovejoy, David S. *Rhode Island Politics and the American Revolution, 1760–1776.* Providence: Brown University Press, 1958.

Lovell, Louise Lewis. *Israel Angell: Colonel of the 2nd Rhode Island Regiment.* New York: Knickerbocker Press (G. P. Putnam's Sons), 1921.

Lowell, Edward J. *The Hessians and the Other German Auxiliaries of Great Britain in the Revolutionary War.* New York, 1884.

Lyman, Eliza B. *A Reminiscence of Newport Before and During the Revolutionary War.* Newport: Milne Printery, 1906.

Macksey, Piers. *The War for America, 1775–1783.* Cambridge: Harvard University Press, 1964.

Mahan, A. T. *The Influence of Sea Power upon History, 1660–1783.* Boston: Little, Brown & Co., 1897.

———. *Major Operations of the Navies in the War of American Independence.* Boston: Little, Brown & Co., 1913.

Main, Jackson Turner. *The Sovereign States: 1775–1783.* New York: New Viewpoints, 1973.

Manucy, Albert. *Artillery through the Ages.* Washington, D.C.: Government Printing Office, 1949.

Marshall, Douglas W., and Peckham, Howard H. *Campaigns of the American Revolution: An Atlas of Manuscript Maps.* Ann Arbor: University of Michigan Press, 1976.

Meng, John J. *D'Estaing's American Expedition, 1778–1779.* New York: American Society of the French Legion, 1936.

Miller, John C. *Triumph of Freedom: 1775–1783.* Boston: Little, Brown & Co., 1948.

Miller, Nathan. *Sea of Glory: The Continental Navy Fights for Independence, 1775–1783.* New York: David McKay Co., Inc., 1974.

Mitchell, Broadus. *Alexander Hamilton.* 2 vols. New York: Macmillan Co., 1957, 1962.

———. *Alexander Hamilton: The Revolutionary Years.* New York: Thomas Y. Crowell Co., 1970.

Montross, Lynn. *Rag, Tag and Bobtail.* New York: Harper & Bros., 1952.

Moore, George H. *Historical Notes on the Employment of Negroes in the American Army of the Revolution.* New York: Charles T. Evans, 1862.

Morris, Richard B. *The Peacemakers.* New York: Harper & Row, 1965.

Munro, Wilfred H. *The Story of the Mount Hope Lands.* Providence: J. A. & R. A. Reid, 1880.

Murray, Thomas H. *General Sullivan and the Battle of Rhode Island.* Providence: American-Irish Historical Society, 1902.

———. *Irish Rhode Islanders in the American Revolution.* Providence: American Irish Historical Society, 1903.

Nell, William Cooper. *The Colored Patriots of the American Revolution.* Boston: F. Wallcutt, 1855.

———. *Service of Colored Americans in the Wars of 1776 and 1812.* Boston: Robert W. Walcott, 1852.

Nelson, William H. *The American Tory.* New York: Oxford University Press, 1961.

Nolan, James Bennett. *Lafayette in America, Day by Day.* Baltimore: Johns Hopkins Press, 1934.

Partridge, Bellamy. *Sir Billy Howe.* New York: Longmans, Greene & Co., 1932.

Perkins, James Breck. *France in the American Revolution.* Boston, 1911.

Polishook, Irwin H. *Rhode Island and the Union, 1774–1795.* Evanston: Northwestern University Press, 1969.

Preston, Howard W. *The Battle of Rhode Island.* Historical Publication Number 1. Providence: State of Rhode Island and Providence Plantations, Office of the Secretary of State, State Bureau of Information, 1928.

Quarles, Benjamin. *The Negro in the American Revolution.* Chapel Hill: published for the Institute of Early American History and Culture, Williamsburg, Virginia, by the University of North Carolina Press, 1964.

Ramsay, David. *The History of the American Revolution.* 2 vols. London: printed for John Stockdale, 1793.

Raymond, Marcius D. *Colonel Christopher Greene.* Tarrytown: Argus Press, 1902.

Rider, Sidney S. *An Historical Inquiry Concerning the Attempt to Raise a Regiment of Slaves by Rhode Island During the War of the Revolution. Rhode Island Historical Tracts,* No. 10. Providence: Sidney S. Rider, 1880.

Sabine, Lorenzo. *Biographical Sketches of Loyalists of the American Revolution.* 2 vols. Boston, 1864.

Sanborn, Nathan. *General John Glover and His Marblehead Regiment in the Revolutionary War.* Marblehead, 1929.

Sears, Lorenzo. *John Hancock: The Picturesque Patriot.* Boston: Little, Brown & Co., 1912.

Smith, Page. *John Adams.* 2 vols. Garden City: Doubleday & Co., Inc., 1962.

———. *A New Age Now Begins: A People's History of the American Revolution.* 2 vols. New York: McGraw-Hill, 1976.

Smith, Paul H. *Loyalists and Redcoats: A Study in British Revolutionary Policy.* Chapel Hill: published for the Institute of Early American History and Culture by the University of North Carolina Press, 1964.

Stedman, Charles. *The History of the Origin, Progress, and Termination of the American War.* 2 vols. London: J. Murray, J. Debrett, & J. Kirby, 1794.

Stember, Sol. *The Bicentennial Guide to the American Revolution.* Vol. I: *The War in the North.* New York: Saturday Review Press, 1974.

Stephenson, Nathaniel Wright, and Dunn, Waldo Hilary. *George Washington.* 2 vols. Oxford University Press, 1940.

Stevens, John Austen. *The French in Rhode Island, Newport in the Revolutionary Period, 1778–1782.* N.p.: Franklin Printing House, 1928.

Stinchcombe, William C. *The American Revolution and the French Alliance.* Syracuse: Syracuse University Press, 1969.

Stone, Edwin Martin. *Our French Allies.* Providence: Providence Press Co., 1884.

Swan, Frank H. *General William Barton.* Providence: Roger Williams Press, 1947.

Taylor, Erich A. O'D. *Campaign on Rhode Island, MDCCLXXVIII.* 6 broadsides. [Newport], n.d. [Reprinted in 1978 in booklet form.]

Thayer, Theodore. *Nathanael Greene: Strategist of the American Revolution.* New York: Twayne Publishers, 1960.

Tuckerman, Henry T. *The Life of Silas Talbot: A Commodore in the Navy of the United States.* New York: J. C. Riker, 1850.

Varnum, J. M. *A Sketch of the Life and Public Services of James Mitchell Varnum.* Boston: David Clapp & Son, 1906.

Wade, Herbert T., and Lively, Robert A. *This Glorious Cause: The Adventures of Two Company Officers in Washington's Army.* Princeton: Princeton University Press, 1958.

Wallace, Willard M. *Appeal to Arms.* New York: Harper, 1951.

———. *Traitorous Hero: The Life and Fortunes of Benedict Arnold.* New York: Harper, 1954.

Ward, Christopher. *The War of the Revolution.* 2 vols. Ed. J. R. Alden. New York: Macmillan Co., 1952.

Ward, John. *A Memoir of Lieut.-Colonel Samuel Ward, First Rhode Island Regiment, Army of the American Revolution: With a Genealogy of the Ward Family.* New York, 1875.

Wertenbaker, Thomas Jefferson. *Father Knickerbocker Rebels: New York City during the Revolution.* New York: Charles Scribner's Sons, 1948.

Whitridge, Arnold. *Rochambeau.* New York: Macmillan Co., 1965.

Whittemore, Charles Park. *A General of the Revolution: John Sullivan of New Hampshire.* New York: Columbia University Press, 1961.

Willcox, William B. *Portrait of a General: Sir Henry Clinton.* New York: Random House, 1964.

Williams, Catherine R. *Biography of Revolutionary Heroes: Containing the Life of Brigadier General William Barton, and also of Captain Stephen Olney.* Providence, 1839.

Winslow, Edward J. *The Hessians and Other German Auxiliaries of Great Britain in the Revolutionary War.* New York, 1884.

Winsor, Justin, ed. *Narrative and Critical History of America.* 8 vols. Boston: Houghton Mifflin & Co., 1884–89.

II. ARTICLES

Amory, Thomas C. "The Siege of Newport." *The Rhode Island Historical Magazine,* V (1884–85), 106–35.

Barnett, Paul. "The Black Continentals." *Negro History Bulletin,* XXXIII (January 1970), 6–10.

Billias, George A. "General Glover's Role in the Battle of Rhode Island." *Rhode Island History,* XIX (April 1959), 33–42.

Boisvert, Donald J. "The Storm That Changed the Course of History." *Yankee,* August 1970, pp. 62–65, 160–64.

Bolhouse, Gladys. "Women and the Battle for Rhode Island." *Newport History,* XLI (Winter 1968), 34–41.

"Boston Riot." *Magazine of American History,* VIII (1882), 785, 856.

"Boston Riot." *Magazine of American History,* XV (1886), 95–96.

Brown, Gerald S. "The Anglo-French Naval Crisis, 1778: A Study of Conflict in the North Cabinet." *William & Mary Quarterly,* XIII (January 1956), 3–25.

Chudacoff, Nancy Fisher. "The Revolution and the Town: Providence, 1775–1783." *Rhode Island History,* XXXV (August 1976), 71–89.

Conley, Patrick T. "The Revolution's Impact on Rhode Island." *Rhode Island History,* XXXIV (November 1975), 121–28.

Dearden, Paul F. "The Siege of Newport: Inauspicious Dawn of Alliance." *Rhode Island History,* XXIX (February–May 1970), 17–35.

"The Destruction of Property in the Town of Middletown, Rhode Island, During the Revolution." *The Newport Historical Magazine,* I (April, 1881), 241–43.

Greene, Lorenzo J. "Some Observations on the Black Regiment of Rhode Island in the American Revolution." *The Journal of Negro History,* XXXVII (April 1952), 142–72.

Greene, Mary A. "Christopher Greene, the Hero of Red Bank." *American Monthly Magazine,* II (May 1893), 521–26.

Lippitt, Charles Warren. "The Battle of Rhode Island." *Bulletin of the Newport Historical Society,* No. 18 (October 1915), pp. 1–14.

Mayer, Lloyd M. "The Battle of Rhode Island." *Bulletin of the Newport Historical Society,* No. 4 (October 1912), pp. 1–7.

———. "New Lights from Old History." *Bulletin of the Newport Historical Society,* No. 87 (April 1933), pp. 1–12.

Powel, H. W. H. "Butt's Hill Fort Celebration, August 29th, 1923." *Bulletin of the Newport Historical Society,* No. 47 (November 1923), pp. 1–22.

———. "Early Defences of Newport During the Siege in 1778." *Bulletin of the Newport Historical Society,* No. 47 (November 1923), pp. 23–24.

Preston, Howard W. "Lafayette's Visits to Rhode Island." *Rhode Island Historical Society Collections,* XIX (1926), 1–10.

———. "Rhode Island and the Loyalists." *Rhode Island Historical Society Collections,* XII (January 1929), 5–10.

Rider, Sidney S. "The Experiences of Rhode Island with Her Negro Troops." *Booknotes,* V (1888), 22–24.

————. "A Review of Field's *Revolutionary Defences.*" *Booknotes,* XVI (1896), 73–75.

————. "A Review of *Warren in the Revolution* by Virginia Baker." *Booknotes,* XVIII (1901), 129–34.

————. "Rhode Island's Negro Soldiers Again." *Booknotes,* V (1888), 62.

Roelker, W. G. and Collins, Clarkson A., III. "The Patrol of Narragansett Bay (1774–1776) by H.M.S. *Rose,* Captain James Wallace." *Rhode Island History,* VII–IX (1948–50), serialized.

Rosengarten, J. G. "The German Soldiers in Newport, 1770–1779." *The Rhode Island Historical Magazine,* VII (October 1886), 76–118.

Shipton, Nathaniel N. "General Joseph Palmer: Scapegoat for the Rhode Island Fiasco of October, 1777." *The New England Quarterly,* XXXIX (December 1968), 498–512.

Skinner, Harriet D. "Newport During the Revolution." *The American Monthly Magazine,* IV (February 1894), 103–17.

"Slaves Enlisted into the Continental Army in 1778." *The Narragansett Historical Register,* I (1882–83), 313.

Smith, Fritz-Henry, Jr. "The French at Boston During the Revolution." *Bostonian Society Publications,* X (1913), 43–49.

Stevens, John Austin. "The French in Rhode Island." *The Magazine of American History,* III (July 1879), 385–436.

Terry, Roderick. "The Story of Green End Fort at the Siege of Newport." *Bulletin of the Newport Historical Society,* No. 51 (October 1924), pp. 7–14.

Thurston, C. R. "Newport in the Revolution." *New England Magazine,* XI (1894), 3–19.

Wilbour, Belinda O. "The Battle of Rhode Island and Some of the Events Preceding It." *The American Monthly Magazine,* III (1898), 228–34.

Willcox, William B. "British Strategy in America, 1778." *Journal of Modern History,* XIX (June 1947), 114–17.

————. "Rhode Island in British Strategy, 1780–1781." *Journal of Modern History,* XVII (December 1945), 304–31.

III. UNPUBLISHED MATERIALS

Carlson, Paul C. "James Mitchell Varnum and the American Revolution." Master's thesis, Wesleyan University, 1965.

Cohen, Joel Alden. "Rhode Island and the American Revolution: A Selective Socio-Political Analysis." Doctoral dissertation, University of Connecticut, 1967.

Dearden, Paul F. "The Rhode Island Campaign of 1778: Inauspicious Dawn of Alliance." Master's thesis, Providence College, 1972.

————. "The Rhode Island Campaign: A Testing Ground of the Franco-American Alliance." Research paper, Providence College, 1969.

————. "The Siege of Newport and the French Alliance." Research paper, Providence College, 1969.

Putnam, Eben. "Notes on Israel Angell." RIHS.

Rhode Island Historical Society. "British Fortifications in Middletown, Rhode Island."

Rudy, Robert Richard. "Rhode Island in the Revolution." Master's thesis, University of Rhode Island, 1958.

Updike, Wilkins. "The Life of General Varnum." Updike Papers. RIHS.

Index